Reviewed 29/05/2005

Roses
in modern gardens

Roses
in modern gardens

Sally Court

MITCHELL BEAZLEY

In memory of my father who, with my mother, created beautiful gardens, loved roses, and introduced me to the artistry of landscaping.

Roses in Modern Gardens

First published in 2004 by Mitchell Beazley,
an imprint of Octopus Publishing Group Ltd, 2–4 Heron Quays, London E14 4JP

ISBN 1 84000 892 X

A CIP record of this book is available from the British Library

Executive Art Editor Sarah Rock
Commisioning Editor Michèle Byam
Editor Selina Mumford
Designer Helen Taylor
Picture Researcher Claire Gouldstone
Production Sarah Rogers
Indexer Sue Farr

Set in Agenda

To order this book as a gift or an incentive contact
Mitchell Beazley on 020 7531 8481

Printed and bound in China by
Toppan Printing Company Limted

Half title: *Miscanthus sinensis* and *Rosa* 'Iceberg' at the Jardin de l'Alchimiste, Eygalières, Provence, France.

Title page: David Austin roses in a design by Alison Armour-Wilson, Chelsea Flower Show 2001.

Contents page "Garden of Transparency", designed by Charles Funke Associates, Chelsea Flower Show 2002.

Contents

I find it bizarre that such a beautiful plant as the rose has been used over the centuries more than any other plant as the emblem for warring countries. The War of the Roses raged for 30 years in the 15th century between the Houses of York (white) and Lancashire (red), where each faction bore the rose as its insignia. For the English it is a patriotic symbol, and it is also the national flower

War of the Roses

of Germany. But this is a divisive plant which continues to cause unrest, albeit on an altogether different plane: the garden. This versatile flower now stirs heated debate across the world, with one faction distinctly against it in modern planting schemes. On the other side are those who believe that the rose has a rightful place in today's gardens and continue to plant it with great pleasure and exuberance.

The drama created by combining the graceful grass *Miscanthus sinensis* 'Variegata' with *Rosa* 'Iceberg' in the contemporary white rose garden at the Jardin de l'Alchimiste, Eygalières, Provence, France has been achieved by the restrained use of colour and plant material, as well as the simplicity of the overall design.

My own early memories of roses are of hybrid teas, climbers, and my father's regular job of pruning. Both my parents were passionate gardeners, and roses were very much part of the mix. My father would spend hours twice a year tackling the prickly problem of pruning back and tying in the branches, emerging with his arms covered with small bleeding wounds. This did not deter him. Soil preparation, regular feeding with well-rotted compost, and pest and disease control produced some very splendid blooms. *Rosa* 'Queen Elizabeth', *R.* 'Peace', *R.* 'Paddy McGredy,' and *R.* 'Iceberg' were among the favourites and, of course, when the vermilion-flowered 'Super Star' (also known as 'Tropicana') was introduced, it found its way into the garden. I can remember my mother bemoaning the fact that its colour made it very difficult to combine well with other plants but nevertheless we had a "hedge" of this along one boundary in the front garden. Another bone of contention was the disappointment with the vivid crimson climbing hybrid tea 'Ena Harkness', whose oversized flower always hung down. These memories are of the 1960s, and over the years my parents' taste changed. In more recent gardens their passion for roses continued, but moved on to old-fashioned

varieties and the new English bush roses from David Austin, which offered much more subtle colours and natural shapes combined with rich perfumes and wondrous flower heads. My mother used to take cuttings from her favourites with some considerable success and add these plants to the borders. Roses have always had a place in her gardens wherever she has lived.

It was in the 1980s when my own interest in roses began. On my first visit to the Chelsea Flower Show I was amazed and excited by the exhibits of the celebrated rose growers Peter Beales and David Austin, and this was well before I qualified as a garden designer. I couldn't wait to start my own garden and grow my favourite climber, *Rosa* 'Mermaid', and scented bushes with a deeply sensuous fragrance combined with rich colours such as *R.* 'Souvenir du Docteur Jamain'. At that time the trend was towards low-maintenance, and roses require a lot of care and attention if they are to flourish.

In the 1990s fashion dictated that roses were passé in many contemporary gardens, and there was a terrific swing towards minimalism. So as a garden designer, like many of my peers, I rarely included them in planting schemes apart from occasionally in traditional mixed borders or in specific rose gardens. However, now there is a fashion for more "wild" or naturalistic gardens I am able to include species roses in my designs and look to nature for my motivation.

There is nothing more inspiring than seeing wild roses in their natural habitats. They are found across the world in their multitude, giving us fresh leaf colour in spring, scent and delicate blooms in summer, and a plethora of

BELOW At Heale House, Wiltshire, Harold Peto's design for the boat terrace incorporated a magnificent balustrade draped with roses. This provides a startling contrast to the giant gunnera leaves that are growing over an old irrigation system, originally installed in 1690 to create a water meadow.

BELOW RIGHT *Rosa* 'Graham Thomas', a strongly scented, deep golden-yellow rose, was bred by David Austin and named after the man who did more than anyone else in the 20th century to reinstate the "old" rose within the plant palette of gardeners and designers alike.

hips and vivid hues in autumn. Once again they are influencing the way in which we are use them in gardens today, but it has taken a while for them to find their way back into our hearts. These simple species lost their attraction when our taste in roses was for the showier, new introductions. Even the old-fashioned shrub and climbing roses fell from grace, only to be replaced in many gardens in the 1950s and 1960s by the hybrid teas and floribundas. At this time, immediately after the World War II, an attitude prevailed to cast away the shadows of the past and these new plants with their classically shaped buds, robust health, and vibrant colours signalled a clearly defined bright future. There is nothing soft about these roses, as they are stripped back to the bare minimum, allowing the flowers to dominate. Sadly, many did not even have that wonderful perfume associated with the rose of old. And, worse still, in their dormant season they required such hard pruning that the plant was left with a collection of bare, ugly sticks protruding above the earth. Unfortunately, this unattractive structure of the hybrid tea also has to be disguised during the flowering season. These strange tortured shrubs do not blend happily in a mixed border or with new perennial planting. Nevertheless, stark borders housing a collection of roses, possibly enclosed by clipped box or lavender, and sometimes inappropriately underplanted with bedding plants and bulbs, continue to appear in public parks and gardens. These uninviting rose collections have probably done more to colour our impression of roses and how to use them than anything else. This, of course, maligns the rose species and is more than a slight sweeping statement. Old-fashioned, scented roses whether climbers or shrubs have always had a place in our hearts and will continue to be there, but their associations are placed firmly in traditional borders, stately homes, and rectories.

In 1902, when William Robinson instructed his gardeners to dig up the west lawn at Gravetye Manor to create a formal rose garden, he caused a great stir

within the gardening fraternity. Only thirty years earlier Robinson had written *The Wild Garden* extolling the virtues of the "sweet unbroken lawn", and was the leader of the informal, naturalistic movement. Yet, here he was creating a garden laid around 46 rectangular beds with rustic pergolas, each planted with a different variety of rose then underplanted with summer bedding in stiff formality. But Robinson was just following the trends in the late Victorian era. Elsewhere in his gardens, he still followed his earlier edicts and a great mound of *Rosa glauca* freely grew in his naturalistic "flower garden", blending with informally planted perennials and shrubs. Robinson was the first great gardener-plantsman, and his writing, garden practices, and ideas, which are still relevant today, continue to influence the way in which we plant.

Unique gardens such as Sissinghurst created by Vita Sackville-West, Monet's Giverny, Beatrix Farrand's design for the sunken rose garden at Dumbarton Oaks, Washington, and the Caetani family's reclaimed gardens at Ninfa, Italy, are probably some of the most influential planting schemes that helped to revive our jaded feelings towards using roses in the garden. These gardens are all masterpieces created in the early 20th century, most of them having a strong sense of structure within the garden. Certainly Gertrude Jeykll's style and a distinct European influence can be found in a large number of gardens that came to life around this time, although many have a very much more

ABOVE *Rosa* 'Ena Harkness', a hybrid tea, originated in Britain in 1946. Although it is considered one of the best crimson flowers, its weak stalks are unable to support its heavy flowers.

OPPOSITE The formality of this garden designed by Dan Kiley is offset by the hybrid tea roses grouped in blocks of colour at its edge.

BELOW Thomas Church used linear geometry in his designs and frequently put raised borders in small gardens to add a vertical dimension. The use of a single plant, the rose, emphasizes the simplicity of his designs.

relaxed grouping of plants than previously found in Victorian gardens. These gardens and the introduction of New English Roses from David Austin have rightly jolted us into reintroducing the rose into the gardens of today.

Many of the great landscape and garden designers of the 20th century used roses in their schemes. Some were routed in tradition, as with Harold Peto's design of the boat terrace and balustrade at Heale House, where roses cascade down towards the water (*see pages 10–11*). This 1911 design of Peto's was formal but perfectly complemented the house, originally built in 1641, with his use of natural materials, plants, and textures. Yet others were experimenting with more radical ideas and going completely against convention.

Until World War I the garden had been perceived as the province of the grand house and landed gentry. Gardens and gardening for the masses had involved, at best, a small vegetable plot with a few flowers. But in general it was a working space. After the 1914–18 war, new houses for the middle classes were being constructed with smaller, more manageable gardens. Nevertheless, the planting often reflected the style of the grander estates until a free-thinker in the United States turned this idea on its head. Thomas Church was the landscape architect who upset this convention by designing gardens for outdoor living. A radical idea that started in his home state of California travelled the length and breadth of the USA and was successfully exported across the world. Gardens and their design were spaces in which the owners play an active role and maintain themselves. Church's designs for these small plots stripped out the unnecessary embellishments of the grander establishment; they incorporated contemporary paving, lawns, and plant material in perfect proportion, always taking into consideration the climate and sustainability of the plants. His gardens appealed to the discerning

masses, and many of his designs included large-scale rose plantings, but he continued to contain them within neatly clipped box borders.

In the mid 1930s this movement came of age in America and was to influence the way in which gardens were to develop over the next decades. It continues to affect the way in which we currently design our gardens. The ringleaders were the radical-thinking landscape architects, Garrett Eckbo, James Rose, and Dan Kiley. Graduates of Harvard Graduate School of Design they stripped their plans down to the simplest of schemes, where clean uncluttered lines ruled, and minimalism was born. Spatial awareness and geometry combined with an inner sense of the landscape evolving from the earth made their designs outstanding. Of the three, only Dan Kiley, to my knowledge, used roses in any of his designs, and the most notable was his "chequerboard" garden at Brentwood, California (*see p.12*), which is now considered to be a modern classic; in his design a huge border is planted up solely with roses.

BELOW A white border can be beautiful but it is also complex to create, as not all whites are pure and, if not carefully selected, can look dull. Here, Ton ter Linden has proved he is master of the art, mixing textures and leaf colour, silvers and whites, to create an illuminating composition.

BELOW RIGHT In the misty morning light a mixed border has a magical feel. The deep black-red of Oriental poppies, huge allium heads, and spires of verbascums, with the roses climbing the mellow brick wall, are all in perfect harmony with each other.

FOLLOWING PAGE Ton ter Linden's borders are reminiscent of the pictures painted by the Impressionists. Colour combinations observed from a distance seem like a whole picture, but when viewed close up are seen as collections of plants arranged in disparate patterns, with textures and colours working together to make the image.

At around the same time another movement – one that has become equally respected and is perhaps adopted as a more harmonious method of creating gardens – was developing in Europe. This was a movement where plants are the main players in the garden. Mien Ruys was a well respected landscape architect with her feet firmly planted in Modernism and the functional approach to garden design. She abhorred unnecessary ornamentation. Although her work became more architectural it was always softened by a rich layer of planting, using a mix of shrubs, roses, beautiful herbaceous plants, and stunning grasses. I feel that this was a feminine approach where a passion for plants and a respect for nature led the design, whereas the American style was much more cutting edge and masculine. Ruys created a style that would take future designers towards "new perennial planting", which today is led by Ton ter Linden, James van Sweden and Wolfgang Oehme, Piet Oudolf, and Christopher Bradley-Hole. Only ter Linden uses roses in his mixed borders. The others are "purists" who do not believe that roses have a place in their herbaceous and grass borders.

It is here that we are beginning to retrace our steps back to nature. A combination of plants in harmony with each other creates a very natural appearance. So, I am not altogether certain why roses do not have a place in these schemes. After all, look at the gardens Dr Miriam Rothschild has created from wild flowers. She has planted species roses in meadow grass on a disused piece of land to make a haven for both wildlife and humans. She has been inspired by nature and sees no reason to use introduced and hybridized plants when there is sufficient wild plant material to create a breathtaking garden. A wild rose *in situ* can be replicated in our interpretation of wild gardens, and it is our responsibility to use roses in conservation and gardens equally.

The formal garden can take on many forms, and today's designers are now breaking the old rules of traditional parterres, renowned at Versailles or Hampton Court Palace. Asymmetry, as seen in the paintings of Miró, Picasso, and their contemporaries, has inspired the new wave of landscape designers to experiment with their schemes. Nevertheless, no matter how far

Contemporary Formality

the boundaries of these plants have been stretched, one of the components that recurs is the rose in its many forms. Roses lend themselves to being planted in formal settings, whether contained within smartly clipped box edging, standing to attention with military precision, or in simple grid patterns echoing the template laid down by the minimalist designer.

Michael Balston's "Best in Show" garden of 1999 at Chelsea, echoed the lines of an ocean liner and used modern materials in conjunction with traditional stone and rich, mixed herbaceous borders to create a truly contemporary garden. The borders were punctuated with the architectural forms of yuccas and phormiums which complemented the softer shapes of roses, viburnums, and cercis, together with an interesting diversity of perennials. This garden has been rebuilt at RHS Wisley, Surrey, but sadly neither the planting nor the hard landscaping have stood up well to the transplantation.

Simplicity, symmetry, and a delineation of specific areas of grass, water, and plants are the ingredients for a formal garden and have been since the earliest known gardens, from the cruciform shape of the paradise gardens of Islam to the more overblown, sumptuous style of the Renaissance. It is a global style that sits as happily in Italy and Britain as it does in New Zealand and South Africa with, of course, regional subtleties. The delight of formality is that the eye can appreciate the clear division between wild countryside and the precision of the man-made garden confined by regulated boundaries. Perhaps the real appeal of the formal layout is that nothing is random, and there is perfect balance. Nevertheless, gardens always evolve, and contemporary formal gardens quite often veer towards Minimalism, many are controversial and quite frequently make us uncomfortable but they always stimulate the senses.

With the modern trend to cut out all unnecessary decoration, sometimes including plants in a garden, the rose has frequently been dumped on the scrap heap. Labelled "old fashioned", and difficult to look after, it is therefore not a plant to be used in this age that demands low maintenance and the latest fashion in the garden. So it is a brave designer who includes roses in a contemporary planting design.

This is a great shame as many of today's roses have long flowering periods from late spring often until midwinter, and lots of them are disease resistant. The colours are mouthwatering, from the richest, deepest almost black-red to the palest of pale shell pinks, sparkling yellows, and cheerful peaches and

BELOW An avenue of clipped box, white roses with tall verbascums, and round-headed alliums leads the eye up the gravel path to the house beyond. The restrained use of colour and the repetition of the same plants provide the path with a simple, calming rhythm.

RIGHT An aerial shot of this garden designed by Tom Stuart-Smith shows how it has been divided into rooms with clipped box; brick and grass paths provide definition, while richly planted borders add colour and texture. The repeat-flowering roses 'Gruss an Aachen', planted in blocks, and Mary Rose in the parterre garden will continue to flower late into the year.

apricots; there is always one that will fit the bill in any planting scheme. Roses
have many good things to offer: from large multi-petalled heads to delicate,
single flowers carrying a central golden crown of anthers; deep velvet colours;
heady scents that tempt you to put your nose right into the blooms; and
wonderful new leaves unfurling in spring. All of these reasons should make us
think of modern planting combinations that utilize this most versatile of
plants. I am equally to blame. Although I do use roses in my designs, more
often than not, they are part of a traditional mixed border, or trained up a
pergola or wall, or within the confines of a formal, box-edged rose garden.
Albeit beautiful, this is hardly cutting edge. I do find that in England many
clients feel uncomfortable whenever modern designs are suggested, and they
take refuge in the safe images of traditional cottage style. We designers are
not, on the whole, good at explaining to clients how a rose can be used in
perfect harmony with a contemporary plan, which will not be at odds with
their needs and the setting. Although contemporary design is gradually being
recognized as an art form by the more sophisticated client what is required is
the work of designers and plantsmen such as Christopher Bradley-Hole and
Piet Ouldof characterized by their wonderful plant combinations and simple

grid layouts. This is all breathtakingly beautiful and quite formal, but to my knowledge, Bradley-Hole usually eschews the use of shrubs let alone roses. Oudolf does use shrubs and clipped hedges to give definition to his gardens, but I don't think I've seen a rose in his plantings.

Thankfully designers such as Tom Stuart-Smith and Arne Maynard both appear to love abundance and sumptuousness in their gardens and include many old and English roses in their schemes. Their work is based on strong formality, with compartments making separate rooms within the garden. These designers do not stint on the plant material used, and roses can be seen in profusion, enhancing the mix in the border, picking up a colour, and creating a theme in the bed. Their style is not part of the minimalist school but firmly rooted in formality. Neither is afraid of using contemporary materials and clean lines in their designs, but always there is a feeling that the plant is equally important than the hard landscaping, if not more so.

The use of clipped box in formal gardens has historical roots. The nature of this evergreen plant means that it can be cut into numerous shapes, so provides a border with a definite shape. The human eye and mind likes clear definition. And when viewed from above, clipped box forms perfect patterns. Other plants are less adaptable, and the form and shape of some of them, particularly if not used in combination with complementary plants, is just ugly. Unfortunately, all roses have been saddled with this misnomer. I agree that the hybrid tea roses that were so overused after the World War II did fall into this category. Their tortured branches set in gnarled rootstock and then pruned within an inch of their life were not sticks of beauty.

LEFT Gunilla Pickard has used low and high hedges to bisect paths and create rooms within this garden. Its modern mix of roses and shrubs makes for a less-structured border, while adhering to the rules of a formal garden with axis and focal points.

ABOVE The rose garden that Sir Miles Warren has planted at Ohinetahi, New Zealand, exemplifies the traditional formal garden, with its neatly clipped topiary box and its columnar yews not only acting as an end stop to the path but also taking the eye up to the spectacular mountains beyond. This is an excellent example of how planting with roses en masse works rather better than a mixed shrubbery, which could not compete against the breathtaking backdrop.

LEFT A simple arch smothered in single white roses with immaculately clipped topiary capturing the light of the evening sun. The shape of the arch is repeated in the topiary and the wooden arbour which can be seen at the end of the vista.

BELOW In France, at the Berquerie in Normandy a long strip of ornamental grass has been planted under the line of yellow roses leading back towards the property. This band of colour gives definition to the edge of the pool planted up with *Iris pseudocorus*.

But old-fashioned shrub roses and David Austin's English roses make attractive shrubs in their own right. Nevertheless, when teamed with harmonizing plants such as box, lavender, or even a dense underplanting of hostas make a wonderful border.

In modern gardens there is still a division between those where roses should be planted as a formal rose garden on their own or as part of a mixed shrubbery. The jury is still out, thank goodness, as there is a place for both of these styles. The mixed shrubbery is a more relaxed, informal style, that perhaps lends itself towards the way in which we now live, while the truly formal rose garden, although sensuous and laden with scented air, is reminiscent of a more autocratic time when everything had a place. Each has its own special beauty. Formality helps strengthen the routes through a garden. These are, generally speaking, linear gardens where the house is

BOTTOM LEFT The artifice of placing an arch at the top of the steps helps separate one part of the garden from the other.

RIGHT Well-placed steps enclosed by lush rose planting encourages the visitor to move through the garden and explore.

OVER PAGE There are few things more beautiful than the evening light playing on a garden; and here it brings a warm glow to the roses on the terraced garden at Somerset Lodge, Petworth. Formal borders are full of centifolia roses, and clipped yew pillars provide a contrast with the nearby fields. Strategically placed benches allow you to stop and enjoy the sensual rose garden.

linked to the garden by a main axis, which forms the backbone. In a large garden there may be several axes and subdivisions leading to smaller more intimate areas or towards a stunning view outside the garden.

Arches are useful devices that can be positioned to connect one area to another, to form paths, and frame vistas. Famous gardens such as the Roseraie de l'Haÿ, Mottisfont Abbey, and Giverny boast many rose arches, all smothered in the most spectacular displays of exuberant flowers. Perhaps these are considered old-fashioned but they still inspire a feeling of well being as you stroll beneath them drinking in their fragrance (the evening is the best time to visit). These gardens have been designed along classical lines, but without the added height from the pergolas and arches an aspect would be lost, leaving the gardens feeling one-dimensional. They help unite the different parts of the garden by not only providing height to the layout but also screening one area from another, thereby creating secret sections beyond to entice visitors to wander through and explore further.

Arches are used for supporting roses and other climbing plants and are mainly found in traditional gardens, but I have noticed a revival in this garden feature with a number of contemporary frames coming on to the market. You only have to look at Kathryn Gustafson's scaffold-pole framework that she has used to support the climbing roses at Terrasson (*see pp.128–9*) to see that unusual and untraditional materials can be used in a rose garden. The simplest ones seem to work best with roses, allowing the plant to be the main performer, and the flowers themselves, the stars.

Avenues and steps all add to the atmosphere of a garden. A change in level can generate a new pace through the garden, a journey towards the next stage. What could be more inviting than a gentle flight of steps flanked by sweet-smelling roses leading one into a different part of the garden?

Cellars-Hohenort Hotel, South Africa

LIZ McGRATH

The gardens of this elegant hotel, situated in the heart of the Constantia Valley, have their origins in the early 1600s when the French Huguenots settled in the region and brought with them their viticultural knowledge. Later, the Dutch East India Company planted this fertile area with vegetables and grapevines to extend the company's gardens. Today, the hotel's landscaped gardens cover 3.7ha (9 acres); they nestle against the densely forested eastern slopes of Table Mountain and have spectacular views of False Bay. The current gardens with their incredible setting have become renowned, especially for their use of roses and indigenous plants. They are made up of a series of rooms and walks that include two specific rose gardens, although a plethora of climbers, ramblers, and shrub roses can be found throughout.

BELOW AND BELOW RIGHT White standard roses form an avenue alongside a box-edged path, while the shrub roses with their contrasting foliage create a carpet of white roses around the white-edged pool to bring unity to the Jardin Blanc.

Liz McGrath is responsible for creating the gardens. She has used peach-coloured shrub roses enclosed by low, clipped box edges to border brick pathways, while simple metal arbours weighed down by climbers look spectacular against the backdrop of Table Mountain. Stiff hybrid tea roses seem to be favoured in the two formal rose gardens, but it is the Jardin Blanc that really stands out as it is more contemporary in its design and limited choice of plants.

It is truly difficult to create an all-white garden. In the White Garden at Sissinghurst the presence of colour helps create the illusion of white throughout, and these bright punctuations give the garden all the more impact. But here, in the Jardin Blanc, the intensity of light against the white of the roses and raised walls, softened only by the grey and yellow foliage, make a powerful contrast against the blue of the sky. No further colours are needed to create an impact.

In northern Europe it is another story. There, grey light can deaden the effect, and local gardeners need to introduce touches of yellows, reds, and oranges to lift the starkness and create the illusion of a white garden. In fact Vita Sackville-West never called her White Garden at Sissinghurst white, she always referred to it as the Pale Garden, as she had filled it with harmonizing colours ranging from creams, greys, silvers, lilacs, blue, and shades of green from acidic to dark. Nevertheless, the overall impression was white so that the garden had the magical effect of coming alive in the evening light. The Jardin Blanc is a formal garden edged by box, with a central metal framework of a series of arches, which in summer is smothered by the vigorous white rambler *Rosa mulliganii*; brick paths leading to the other garden rooms radiate from here.

Private garden, Spain

ARABELLA LENNOX-BOYD

The natural ecology of the countryside around this property was highly influential in the way that the design took shape. It provided the inspiration, and the landscaping had to pay homage to the rather severe beauty of the hills beyond. The balance between the wild countryside and the tamed, managed garden was essential to the success of the scheme.

Perfect symmetry is one of the key ways of bringing harmony and balance to a formal garden, as illustrated by this courtyard. A simple cruciform pool, fed by a rill set centrally in a cobbled terrace designed by Arabella Lennox-Boyd, is a lesson in restraint and sophistication. Following rules laid down by the Moors, with four borders placed at the corners of the pool and the architectural spires of cypress trees framing the view, the garden is totally understated with its muted colours blending into each other. Grey foliage plants and evergreens, together with the magnificent white roses, thrive in this sun-drenched garden.

The house is blanketed with a mass of climbing and rambling roses, turning the façade into a Moorish tapestry. Blocks of lavender and the ubiquitous cypress trees anchor the house to the ground and provide essential evergreens to give permanent structure throughout the year. The spectacular display of roses in full bloom not only offers a sense of shade to cool the interior of the house but also engulfs the house with glorious fragrance.

BELOW A rill-fed cruciform pool is the central feature in the White Garden planted with *Pittosporum tobira* and the pure white 'Iceberg' roses.

RIGHT In countries where water is scarce only very hardy roses such as *Rosa* 'Guinée', *R.* 'Madame Grégoire Staechelin', and *R.* 'Desprez à Fleurs Jaunes' can be grown up houses.

The Château de Reux is the epitomy of a romantic Normandy moated castle, set in gardens filled with shrubs and popular roses in pastel colours, such as *Rosa* 'New Dawn' and *R.* 'Iceberg', to soften chilly and severe stone walls and paths. The overall design for the château gardens are formal with clipped yew hedges, low box edgings, and pleached hornbeam rooms and walks. Formality lends itself to simplicity, and brings about a sense

Château de Reux, France

ARABELLA LENNOX-BOYD

of unification and harmony throughout the gardens. When Arabella Lennox-Boyd designed the gardens for the Dovecote Garden, she used *R.* 'Penelope' as the predominant feature in the formal borders that radiate off the cobbled paths. The warm colour of the roses harmonizes with the honey colour of the

LEFT *Rosa* 'Penelope', the fragrant hybrid musk, is one of the best repeat-flowering shrub roses of its class. Bearing large trusses of creamy-pink flowers, followed by coral-pink hips, under the right conditions it can reach 1.8 x 1.8m (6 x 6ft).

BELOW LEFT The warm, natural stone walls and grey, domed roof of the garden building, harmonize with the grey and silver foliage of the planting and the creamy-pink flowers of the roses dominating the planting.

BELOW The large flower trusses of *Rosa* 'Penelope' create magnificent-coloured statements to the exits of the paths. They form a frame to the vista below and beyond the rose border. Honey-coloured cobbles in the path draw the eye straight to the formal pool and clipped hedges below.

local stone used for the garden buildings and paths. Lennox-Boyd, Italian by birth, manages to introduce a strict formality that can be found in great Italian gardens. She brings symmetry and balance to the garden by the use of a central axis, with subdivisions by way of grass crossways and deep borders, level changes, and vistas. The garden slopes gently down to a pool and an enclosed garden in a formally clipped hedge, with the greater hillside view glimpsed in the distance.

Lennox-Boyd adds a touch of warmth and vibrancy by introducing a statement of colour that may have been lost had she used a white-flowering rose combined with the grey- and silver-leafed foliage of the herbaceous border. It could so easily have become one of a number of white rose gardens using a formula repeated in many formal gardens – quite beautiful in itself but nothing out of the ordinary. By choosing *R.* 'Penelope', Lennox-Boyd has introduced not only a fragrant rose but also good flower colour over a long season; there is also the added bonus of hips appearing in autumn and lengthening the interest in the border to at least nine months.

owhere is the Italian influence on modern gardens more in evidence
than here in Tuscany at the Villa il Roseto (the Rose Garden). Pietro
Porcinai, landscape architect and son of the famous Villa Gamberaia's
gardener, was initiated at an early age into the art of formal Italian
gardens. His work here is considered to be the best example of a modern
interpretation of a Renaissance garden. Porcinai, an exponent of the
Florentine Humanist tradition, used this to great effect when he interpreted
his clients' requirements.

Villa il Roseto, Italy

PIETRO PORCINAI

The garden is on many levels, with suspended box parterres and a circular
concrete fish pool built over a covered parking area. Large stretches of mown
lawn, bisected by concrete paths and bordered by a massed planting of a
single-coloured hedge of roses, snake up the hillside, over contoured ground
towards the house. Clipped hedges obscure the views and hide staircases
as well as subdivide the garden, creating secret areas worthy of exploring.
A small path winds down to a magnificent rose garden that gives the property
its name and continues across olive fields and walkways planted with lavender,
wild flowers, and climbing roses. Again, great restraint in material and plant
use has turned this garden into one of quiet, understated magnificence.

LEFT The 17th-century Villa il Roseto painted in a warm colour wash is set on the hilltop with panoramic views of Tuscany. It is named after the countless roses planted within its grounds. Many paved walks wind up the hillside lined with colourful flowers.

ABOVE Tall hedges bisect the hillside and follow paths through the gardens, leading to the rose garden. Whole banks of a single species of pale-pink rose provide definition, while adding colour to the cooling greens of the grass and hedges.

Traditional mixed borders have fallen out of fashion since the early 1990s and replaced with modern perennial planting. The American designer Topher Delaney once claimed "Gertrude Jekyll is dead", and that it is time to move on. However, there is still a lot to learn from the designers of the old school. Vita Sackville-West, Rosemary Verey, Christopher Lloyd, and Penelope Hobhouse

Mixed Borders

turned the mixed border into an art form – Nori and Sandra Pope address today's needs. They, too, understand the way in which to place plants with contemporary colours and textures, and take great pleasure in often introducing roses into the mix which should make more of us rethink our prejudices. They also use traditional methods of planting, including staking rose branches to the ground to encourage low growth.

David Stevens, a designer with a reputation for using bold and sometimes brash colours, is not frightened of having a mixture of clashing colours in his borders. Not to everyone's taste, *Rosa* 'Festival', used in combination with bright yellows and pinks is softened slightly by introducing the mauves of hebes and nepeta in his garden seen at the 1996 Hampton Court Flower Show.

Although there is intense beauty in a minimalist border with the use
of just one colour or plant or type of plant to draw your attention to
a particular feature in the garden, I find the sheer exuberance of a well-
balanced mixed border terrifically exciting. Border structure is enhanced
by the addition of shrubs and evergreens. It is all very well to plant a border
in the new perennial style, as implemented by Piet Oudolf, Noel Kingsbury,
and Christopher Bradley-Hole, but these end up looking very sad and soggy
during the long winter months when we need cheering up.

Here, I need to define what I mean by the term "mixed border". To me, it is a
border that contains a balance of trees, shrubs, perennials, and bulbs, with the
addition of annuals if desired; it may also include vegetables, legumes, salad
leaves, and fruit trees. It may be monochrome, relying on texture and a limited
selection of shades, or it may be full of bright colour provided by flowers and
foliage. It can be narrow or wide, single or double, formal or informal, but it
must contain a mixture of shrubs and herbaceous plants.

In a mixed border there is something new to see at all times of the year,
from the earliest blossom of *Prunus autumnalis* and tough little bulbs, into
spring, when brave new shoots start to appear, almost too quickly followed
by a mass of flower colour, when the shrubs disappear into the background
and let the herbaceous perennials take centre stage. Then, on to autumn,
when the colours turn to magnificent golds, reds, and bronzes to combine
with those late shows of Michaelmas daisies and helianthus, and fountains
of dying grasses with their resplendent flower heads.

BELOW LEFT A mixed border at the Old Manor, Hemingford Grey, Cambridgeshire, with brightly coloured roses and deep blue delphiniums, is filled with complementary shapes. Tall spires contrasting with round flower forms are brought into beautiful relief in the evening sunlight.

BELOW This dramatic border is brought to life by the use of white *Rosa* 'Iceberg', underplanted with nepeta, the bright foliage of *Acer palmatum* 'Atropurpureum', and the acid yellow of the robinia acting like a shaft of sunlight on what could have easily been a gloomy walk.

When a rose is added to this mix, further excitement is to be found as fresh, tender, red leaves start to emerge from the stems, quickly followed by flower buds; almost too soon the blossoms appear to provide us with a sensual bloom steeped with perfume, and then they fade and drop. But they pay dividends. Unlike most of their companion plants in the border, many roses flower time and time again; some bravely keep going until midwinter. What better shrub could be included in this heady mix of plants to keep important colour in the border through so many seasons?

The versatility of the rose means that it can be combined in numerous styles of border. In an informal, cottage-style garden that is found at an old rectory in southeast England herbaceous perennials are allowed to spill over and soften the hard edges of the gravel paths, while shrub roses at the rear of the border arch right over, almost meeting the border on the far side of the path.

Enthusiastic exponents of using roses in the border include great English gardeners such as Penelope Hobhouse and the late Rosemary Verey. In her book *Good Planting*, Verey discussed the argument as to whether roses should stand alone, the purists' theory, or be used in more diverse ways. It is obvious that her feelings were very much towards the latter. Her delight in using roses as part of the groundcover mix in all manner of situations, from densely planted borders alongside a vegetable garden to lining a path, was always creative. She reasoned that if the ground were well prepared then roses would

RIGHT On an old stone wall a pink-flowering climbing rose creates a vertical statement and adds much-needed height to the border. It also provides a sense of scale.

FAR RIGHT This deep border has a profusion of roses ranging from pale through to the deepest pink. The smattering of apricot is muted by the silver-grey of stachys, which almost hides the summerhouse from view. This colourful show should last from early to late summer.

be low-maintenance and an essential part of the border. Not only would they add a long season of colour that complement, contrast with, or enhance delicate perennials and foliage, but they would frequently add structure and an intensity that only a handful of other plants could replicate. There are few shrubs that can surpass the rose, with its first unfurling leaf buds in early spring through to brightly coloured autumnal hips. They make the perfect foil in a mixed border with their rich velvety blooms and textures. Hobhouse can make a convincing case for using roses in the mixed border, from the sophisticated Tudor borders at Hatfield House, Hertfordshire, where only plants from that period are featured, to informal cottage plantings.

Roses look equally at home in formal borders, where the plants are enclosed by geometric paths or clipped box, as seen in garden designer Arne Maynard's own garden in the Fens, eastern England. Here he has created a modern rose garden. Maynard has grown old-fashioned, scented varieties such as *Rosa* 'Fantin-Latour', and underplanted them with old stalwarts including *Geranium* 'Johnson's Blue', sulphur-green euphorbias, and campanulas.

The whole garden, now a series of rooms, has a timelessness about it as well as a feeling of serenity. Although the plan pays tribute to garden history, it is not lost in the past and feels quite contemporary. Above all, his rose garden is very special, with its serpentine hedges, and where pink, purple, blue, and bronze colouring complements trained pyramids of copper beech. Maynard's garden shows an inspired use of traditional plant material with a twist. Designing with passion and sensitivity, he cleverly connects the gardens to the fields beyond.

On a grander scale, at a French château on the River Loire, I have seen roses growing in borders with vegetables, flowers for cutting, and step-over fruit trees, making the most charming eclectic mix, and very colourful magnet for honey bees and a mass of butterflies and other insects. This certainly made me rethink how I was going to plan any future parterre-style gardens. I had never heard or seen a garden so alive with insect life, and I am sure that the regional honey producers were delighted with this local influence.

Roses can also be included very successfully in borders in small gardens,

ABOVE LEFT One of today's most popular climbers, *Rosa* 'New Dawn' was introduced in 1930 as a repeat-flowering sport of *R.* 'Doctor W. Van Fleet'. Vigorous and hardy, the first "modern" climbing rose that marked the start of many repeat-flowering climbers.

FAR LEFT Penelope Hobhouse has combined the hot colour of *Geranium psilostemon* with the more muted pinks and yellows of the roses, deep-blue delphiniums, and pale blue *G.* x *cantabrigiense* to make this combination come to life.

LEFT A superb colour combination of peaches, apricots, and pinks, with dark-green foliage, makes an exciting picture. The planting is made even more interesting in the choice of plants, with *Rosa* 'Sweet Dream' and *Diascia* 'Salmon Supreme' mixed with the frothy heads of heuchera, which contrast with the stiff leaves of phormium.

OVER PAGE Here are hot colours for the heat of the Californian summer. Garden designer Bob Clarke has used jewel colours to create this sensational border by mixing deep pinks with a salmon-coloured rose, interspersed with annuals and biennials: lime green nicotiana, yellow snapdragons, blue forget-me-nots, and the self-seeding Californian poppy.

whether in a town or the countryside, especially if you are a little courageous in what you use in the mix. Choose strong colours to create a vibrancy and enclosure around a small courtyard, or architectural plants to provide a stark contrast to the softer shapes of roses and perennials. Experimentation has always been part of the art of gardening.

I have found in my own tiny patch that roses need a lot of care and attention. I do not like using chemicals in my garden but in the part of London where I live roses seem to get ravaged by black spot, mildew, and rust. Greenfly and sawfly seem to home in on my poor plants and ravish them. Sadly, I have had to resort to spraying with pesticides. The spray, combined with heaps of well-rotted farmyard manure, seems to keep my roses relatively happy. I am not sure whether it is the nature of living in a town that has created the problem of pests and diseases or if man has brought it on. Nevertheless, we should not be daunted by the work involved in maintaining our roses.

Artists-turned-garden designers including such as the British designers Jill Billington and Barbara Hunt know how to combine colours to make their borders make an impact, while Bonita Bulaitis uses new hard-landscaping materials in the most innovative ways, and Christopher Bradley-Hole makes us reconsider our use of perennials. I have not yet come across a designer, owner, or plantsperson who has used roses in the mixed border in a truly cutting-edge, contemporary way, myself included. The exception to this might be Nori and Sandra Pope at Hadspen House, Somerset, (*see pp.54–5*), where they introduced roses to great effect in their colour borders.

ABOVE A 1974 McGredy introduction, bred in New Zealand, *Rosa* 'Dublin Bay' has become one of the world's most widely grown modern climbers due to its adaptation to both hot and cold climates. Loved for its rich, dark velvety flowers and dark green foliage, it is considered to be a perfect rose apart from its one failing, no fragrance.

OPPOSITE In temperate climates warm colours can be used in borders, but they have to be subtle to work in grey light. Here, *Rosa* 'Red Blanket' has been teamed with *Astrantia* 'Hadspen Blood', *A. maxima*, and a vibrant green native fern.

RIGHT The colour of the golden hop in the background helps illuminate *Rosa* 'Festival', *Lychnis coronaria*, and verbascum. This combination is one of glorious vibrancy, with the rich velvety tones of the rose, almost a black-red, being uplifted by the lighter cerise of the lychnis and bright sulphur of the hop.

LEFT This garden designed by Tessa Hobbs is a muted collection of pastel shades with the white stem of the birch and the roses providing a bright contrast to the dark yew hedge enclosing the garden. Mellow red bricks and York stone paving relate well to the traditional mix of lavenders, pinks, salvias, alliums, and the pale-pink rose smothering the archway.

ABOVE Rosa 'Nathalie Nypels', a fragrant dwarf polyantha, has been planted to the front of a border with salvias and Phormium 'Clarissa'.

It takes brave people to develop and manage a garden that since the 17th century has been in the capable hands of many generations of dedicated gardeners, the last of which was no less a plantsperson than Penelope Hobhouse. But husband and wife team Nori and Sandra Pope are passionate gardeners with an innate sense of colour and vast plant knowledge who have more than met this challenge. Throughout its history the garden had suffered long periods of deterioration, the last after Penelope Hobhouse moved on to develop another garden. After eight years of neglect in 1987 the Popes, designers and nurseryfolk from Vancouver Island in Canada arrived, fell in love with the place, recognized its potential, and started to restore the gardens.

Their trademark is the use of colour – at Hadspen they have practised their art to the full and used pure, bold applications of colour in simple unifying tapestries of plants. They have planted the 800m- (½ mile-) long borders in a

Hadspen House, England
NORI & SANDRA POPE

series of colour movements linked by repeated themes, often using a rose to create intensity. Shrub roses have been used throughout the mixed borders and gardens, while ramblers are trained into the beech hedges, and climbers such as *Rosa* 'Leverkusen' are pegged to the ground, where the flowers can mingle at a lower level. However, it is perhaps the transformation of the old vegetable garden for which the Popes are most famous. It is in here, protected by the curved mellow brick walls that their colourful borders almost render the viewer speechless. The extraordinary colour combinations range from the deepest plum hues through to reds and pinks, peaches and oranges, to the brightest yellows; an awe-inspiring progression of plants grouped together by colour tonality from both flowers and foliage. The Popes have not been lured into adding a touch of contrasting colour to temper the borders – all the chosen plants are harmonious. Look at the grouping of yellows, with *Rosa* 'Graham Thomas' and *R.* 'Golden Wings' clustered with *Digitalis lutea*, *Calendula* 'Pacific Apricot', and *Potentilla recta pallida*, to understand the impact that a monochrome border can bring to the garden.

After listening to a lecture given by Nori, I was inspired and could see the logic of using purity in colour for a spectacular result; however I also heard him say that to achieve and maintain this was a huge investment in time and money. This garden perhaps best exemplifies how to choose simplicity over a hotchpotch of uncoordinated plants.

LEFT The sheltered brick wall is smothered with climbing roses, while the delicate *Crambe cordifolia* flowers dancing in the background contrast with the tall spires of foxgloves. The colours are picked up by the creamy-white flowers of *Rosa* 'Sally Holmes', a hardy, repeat-flowering shrub that will provide a long season of colour.

ABOVE Pink is supposed to be a comfortable colour with which to live, but here shock treatment is part and parcel of the pink border. The combination of *Rosa* 'Tuscany Superb' with *Geranium psilostemon*, *Lychnis coronaria*, and *R.* 'William Shakespeare' provides a startling yet imaginative mix set centrally within this border.

How many times have we passed a native hedgerow or walked along a seashore and admired the way in which nature has placed plants. No clashes of colour, wonderful leaf textures, and spectacular blossom. A harmonious mix with which we are at ease. There are a number of gardens that have captured this relationship of garden, nature, and the landscape.

Naturalistic Planting

A balance has been introduced between the naturalistic planting style and the requirements of a garden, and this is strictly maintained. The unique combination of introducing the "wild" into the constraints of the garden set within a boundary, without it appearing messy or contrived is a great skill, and one that we should study. The gardens work because the structure is strong and the plants chosen are in harmony with the environment.

Rosa moyesii, R. 'Albertine', and R. 'Veilchenblau' clustered together make a spectacular show of colour against the dark backdrop of trees on the hillside at La Roseraie de Berty, France, where massed roses have been planted to blur the boundaries of the garden and the natural landscape.

Naturalistic Planting

BELOW Designer Miranda Holland-Cooper has
successfully used *Rosa* 'Marguerite Hilling', a
modern shrub rose with simple, semi-double,
pink flowers, which forms large rounded
bushes when left to naturalize. This is a sport
of *R.* 'Nevada', and, like its parent, requires
rigorous pruning of old wood if it is to
maintain its shape and performance.

OPPOSITE At the Old Manor, Hemingford
Grey, Cambridgeshire, *R. gentiliana*, with its
single white flowers held above the growth,
forms a dark tunnel with the bright light
ahead beckoning the visitor to explore
the garden beyond.

While wandering along an inlet on San Juan Island in the Pacific North
West in late summer, I came across a great show of colour when I
stumbled upon a shower of huge, bright red hips from a native species rose
spilling right over the water's edge. I could not help thinking of my own native
roses in Britain gamely providing a similar show of hips and haws in equally
inclement areas. In addition, their earlier displays of delicate flowers have a
beauty that, when compared to their blousy cousins, is unsurpassed. The
creamy-white burnet rose, found in the shallow dunes and grassy sand hills
around our coast, and the dog rose, with its flat, large, pale pink petals
happiest on scrubland and in hedgerows brighten the most inhospitable
landscapes. The white field rose, which incidentally is almost always located
in woodland, grows across England and Wales with the soft and harsh downy-
roses, and has blossoms ranging from bright pink through to white. All these
species roses attract insect and bird life in great abundance, and their hips are
beneficial to man and beast alike.

Learning from nature is the greatest help to us when we are planning a
naturalistic garden. The wonderful species roses to be found throughout the
world provide clues of where and how to place them within a garden
environment, although they, themselves, would not necessarily be the right
plant for the design. There are purists among us who fervently believe that
only native species should be used in naturalistic gardens but in my opinion
this is too narrow a view. What we should do is study the native habitat of

plants because by imitating nature it is possible to create a garden with a "sense of place". Why restrict ourselves? Why not combine native plants and their hybrids with plants from the rest of the world that survive in the same hardiness zone? Today, we have such a wonderful palette of plants that it would be restricting not to be able to use them. Nevertheless, I am not an advocate of using all and sundry just because they are available, and would recommend that we do curb our enthusiasm; restraint should be exercised at all times if good design is applied. The old adage of "less is more" is a good rule to follow.

In the naturalistic garden, the true plantspeople come to the fore. It is relatively easy to design a formal garden – you cannot really go wrong with a clipped box hedge around a grouping of English shrub roses – but it is more difficult to cluster and place roses in an informal manner. The great Victorian gardener and writer William Robinson was probably one of the earliest reactionaries in the gardening world to use roses in an informal way. He used a limited selection of ramblers and noisette roses together with the species roses, with their simple forms, in his wild gardens and it was this style that probably did more than any other to influence modern gardeners and designers in their use of roses in today's gardens. Luckily, we now have a greater selection of roses from to choose, so we do not have to battle with the unruly growth and die-back existant in Robinson's day.

Roses need a good light source and fertile soil to allow them to develop into attractive natural shapes, mounds, fountains, or pillars. Today, our main problem is space. A rose used in a wild setting needs a lot of room to look its best. A minimum of 0.4ha (1 acre) is required, preferably considerably more; consideration of the gardens of Landriana, Italy, makes apparent the space required to create a sustainable rose garden (*see pp.88–93*). This really rules

LEFT *Rosa moyesii* and its cultivars create a splash of colour in both summer and autumn, with single, blood-red, geranium-shaped flowers followed by an abundance of hips. This large shrub rose, which reaches over 2.5m (8ft) high, is found naturally in the wild in China. Here, it links the old grey-stone walls to the margin of the fields beyond.

BELOW In Beth Chatto's famous gardens, she has blended the repeat-flowering *Rosa* x *odorata* 'Mutabilis', an old China rose, with naturalized planting. The lovely reddy-green foliage harmonizes with the cool mix of colours from white foxgloves, pale lemon verbascums, and sulphur-yellow euphorbia combined with mauve-pinks and greys.

Although confined by a low-clipped box
hedge, tall columnar Irish yews, and orderly
box spheres, the wild atmosphere created
here at Bryan's Ground, Herefordshire,
by the nepeta, fennel, and creamy-yellow
shrub roses set against the huge tree line,
is a case of strict formality constraining
wild informality. It shows a clever contrast
of two styles working together, which is
reminiscent of Tudor parterres.

out anyone with a small town garden who may passionately want to create a wilderness of their own. Additionally, to maintain a naturalistic garden a lot of time and effort needs to be applied. If neglected for even a short period, a naturalistic rose garden will just run to rack and ruin, perhaps turning into an eyesore. Of course, this applies to any "wild" garden whether it has roses or not; all are very labour intensive if the integrity of the design is to be kept. Conversely, for those prepared to put in a huge labour of love and investment in time, the result should definitely be worth it. There is no garden that is more beautiful, more sensual, or more evocative than a wild rose garden.

A well-designed, naturalized garden should have the appearance of the countryside, borrowed and moved into the garden. Although contrived, it should not feel that any planning or effort has been applied. The plants must look as though they have been on the site for ever, rather than deliberately placed. The whole effectiveness of the garden will hang on the choice of roses; if they are too gaudy they will shout at you; too hybridized and they will look out of context; blooms too large or too fussy will also appear out of place. Single flowers or simple shapes are preferable. Paler colours, or those that echo colours found in wildflowers and in season, also blend more sympathetically into a naturalized setting. Ramblers such as 'Kiftsgate', 'Rambling Rector', 'Blush Rambler', and *Rosa banksiae* 'Lutea' are ideal for sprawling up old buildings and trees, while species such as *R. xanthina* and *R. hugonis* with their single yellow blooms look superb set in grass or along a hedgerow. Other species, including *R. glauca* with its stunning stem colour and foliage, or *R. moyesii* with rich blood-red flowers and golden stamens, make wonderful statements planted en masse flanking a pathway. All these roses echo those found in the countryside and create the right feeling of "borrowed landscape".

For gardens true to the wild, naturalistic landscape we only have to look at the work of Dr Miriam Rothschild, whose own garden at Ashton Wold is one of the most awe-inspiring, untamed, and naturalized gardens in the world. Since inheriting the house and "perfect" Edwardian gardens over 40 years ago, she has spent the intervening years working on the latter. It was not until many years later that Rothschild began its metamorphosis. A purist at heart,

Helen Dillon's garden in Dublin combines an exuberant choice of plants. The mixture of *Rosa glauca* and *Hedysarum coronarium* creates a fiery corner of naturalized planting. The deep rich tone of the French honeysuckle is picked up by the stems of the rose, while its blue-grey leaf colour helps to moderate the vibrancy.

BELOW Dr Miriam Rothschild has planted
an avenue of dog roses set in a wildflower
meadow in an abandoned airfield. A stand
of poplars marks the boundary between
the highly naturalized planting and the
tamed landscape.

BELOW RIGHT At Hardwick House in
Cambridgeshire a mown grass path between
an avenue of clipped box shapes, *Rosa
cantabrigiensis*, and the birch set in long
grass creates a formal, minimalist pattern,
which is totally at ease with the countryside.

she has allowed the gardens to revert to the wild, encouraging native wild flowers and grasses to thrive; these, in turn, attract the native fauna to return in their hordes, although parts of the original garden and earlier introductions have been retained. Rothschild's early memories are of permanent southwesterly breezes making the house blinds creak, and there was no bird song to be heard. It is all very different today. Native plants such as wild roses and the vigorous rambler *Rosa* 'Kiftsgate' vie with old man's beard, ivy, wisteria, broom, and a multitude of other rampant plants. The climbing *R.* 'Etoile de Hollande' and *R.* 'Cedric Morris', both early flowering roses, have been planted with wild honeysuckle and white jasmine over the back wall of her long greenhouse, as she cannot resist the "seduction of May roses"; *R.* 'Irish Fireflame', now 90 years old, and the last surviving rose planted by her mother, still flowers along the kitchen garden wall, and an unnamed, rampant white rambler is allowed to grow untamed along a new fence.

A new garden, Jenningsbury at Hertford Green, England, has recently been created by Julie Toll, one of Britain's leading experts in creating and managing meadow and wildflower gardens. Jenningsbury is one of the most spectacular, captivating wild gardens to be found today. It is a restful place, where contrasts between neatly mown grass and wild plantings and rampant, single-flowered roses form a breathtaking picture in early summer.

The lesson learnt is that when working with nature you have to work with scale and understand the unique qualities of the site. Nature is bold, and plants repeat themselves. When balance is achieved between the garden and the countryside in Rothschild's words "the wild garden brings heart's ease".

This rose garden, created from terraces nestling among the wild beauty of steeply wooded slopes, is not strictly speaking a "naturalized" garden as it contains around 600 species, varieties, and cultivars of old roses. Yet for me, by its very nature, its location, and the way in which the roses have been planted – each specimen shown to its own advantage yet never losing sight of the awe-inspiring landscape encircling the garden – makes it a wonderful naturalized garden. No rose later than 1920 has been included in this amazing collection, and each has been selected for its colour, form, texture, and scent.

Roseraie de Berty, France

ELÉONORE CRUSE AND CHRISTIAN BIETTE

The garden began its incarnation when Eléonore Cruse purchased the old farmhouse and land back in 1970. The transformation was a slow process; the garden began life as a small holding and vegetable plot, which helped to enrich the poor soil conditions. Slowly, rare plants were introduced with a few choice roses among the vegetables. Gradually, the balance changed with roses becoming the predominant feature. The gardens are, in the main, cultivated organically, with the incorporation of manure for new plants rather than chemical fertilizers. Cruse's holistic approach to gardening – companion planting to keep predators and diseases at bay – together with a well-judged respect for nature, and an innate ability to design with plants has created one of the most intoxicating gardens in Europe. Today, she is regarded as one of our leading rose specialists, and her methods of cultivation and rose collection are esteemed worldwide.

RIGHT Although this is a completely naturalistic garden, clipped box and yew are used for structure, and help create secret areas that nestle behind roses as tall as trees.

FAR RIGHT In this garden, constructed from terraces on several levels, roses tumble over the natural stone walls rebuilt by Christian Biette. The roses have been allowed to naturalize and have often spread to their neighbours, thus creating a wonderfully rich tapestry of warm colours.

OVER PAGE There appear to be no boundaries to this garden; the natural, densely wooded landscape beyond is anchored to the garden by the use of cypress, with indigenous trees framing the massed planting of old varieties of roses and fountains of grasses.

Urn Cottage, England

LESLEY ROSSER

Garden designer and writer Lesley Rosser has created a quintessential English cottage garden at her home in Gloucestershire. Yet look closely, and it is possible to see that although she has used many traditional flowers and plants associated with a cottage garden, she has concentrated on the new perennial planting style mixed with roses. Her garden is situated in one of the most beautiful parts of England and has views across to fields that enable her to use the landscape as part of the design.

Practitioners of new perennial planting have diverse views as to what should or should not be planted in association with grasses. Piet Oudolf, in his book *Designing with Plants,* co-written with Noel Kingsbury – both renowned exponents of new perennial planting – is adamant that "on the whole, grasses, do not make successful companions for roses." He feels that "there is too much of a contradiction between the intensely gardenesque nature of most roses and the wild beauty of grasses." Perhaps this is a masculine approach to the form and combination of plants. For me, soft fountains of grass flower heads complement roses. Their subtlety offsets the complexity of the rose flower head, while their colours harmonize with each other.

Rosser has used the delightful *Rosa* Bonica in her scheme. This is a modern, repeat-flowering shrub rose with a tidy habit of reaching no more than 1.5m (5ft) in height. Its semi-double, small, pink flowers and dark leathery leaves are relatively disease free, so it gives little trouble and is free flowering. It is also ideal for planting in a naturalized scheme, as the flowers resemble species roses. Rosser has used it in combination with *Potentilla recta pallida*, yellow-flowering achilleas, and *Stipa tenuissima* to provide an idyllic combination of pastel colours that will last right into autumn. There are no hard colours to jar the senses. You only have to look at Eléonore Cruse's use of grasses at the Roseraie de Berty (*see pp.68–9*) to see the effectiveness of combining these two disparate plant species.

In a sheltered corner, Rosser has placed a terrace alongside a wooden pergola smothered in climbing roses, so that when it comes to relaxing she and her family can drink in the heady scents while enjoying an alfresco meal. Nevertheless, Rosser does not want to lull the senses totally as she has used the vibrantly coloured *Rosa* 'Fountain' mixed with acid greens and yellows in the border that links the garden to the fields. This rose is a wake-up call; it is a medium-sized, modern shrub rose, with hybrid tea-shaped flowers with rich blood-red petals that resemble velvet – a fragrant rose that invites you to touch and smell it. Her use of this startling colour at this juncture of the garden makes one stop and take stock of the surroundings before one's gaze drifts out towards the greater countryside. This tactic is used to a greater extent in countries where the light is bright and can reflect the intensity with sizzling effect but in temperate climates it can really liven up a dull corner.

La Ferriera Pescia Fiorentina, Italy

CONTESSA GIUPPI PIETROMARCHI

Garden writer, Helena Attlee, a friend of the Contessa Giuppi Pietromarchi, commented that "there is no horticultural tradition left in Italy", which is why she is in awe of the amazing transformation this determined woman has made of a derelict old iron foundry at Grosseto in Tuscany. Although gardening was in her family's blood, it was not until the Contessa and her husband took on the challenge of this neglected estate with its ancient olive grove and *Pinus nigra* subsp. *maritima* planted with military precision, that she started gardening in earnest. It has taken over 30 years to tame this land and transform the abandoned fields into an inspired and beautiful garden.

The garden reflects her many interests and travels with her husband, a diplomat whose work took them all over the world, is full of treasures picked up en route. However, it is her creation of a rose garden that is a true revelation. Tuscany is a hostile environment for roses, and the gardens at La Ferriera are no exception. Although the soil is a fertile clay, an ideal growing medium for roses, in hot climates it is liable to dry out and become compacted, at which point not even the most resilient plant will survive. The Contessa has improved the soil by adding huge quantities of manure and composts, and has even resorted to removing and replacing soil in her battle to maintain her gardens. An irrigation system, essential in the summer months, draws up muddy water from a river running below her fields. But even this is a problem as the filters have to be cleaned once a fortnight, otherwise the grit carried in the water will damage the pipework. Trial and error has proved that China and noisette roses are best suited to this gruelling climate. A lesser soul would have given up years ago but the Contessa is made of sterner stuff; her efforts have all been worthwhile as in early summer the roses bloom in profusion.

TOP LEFT The "perfect" white rose, 'Iceberg' has become synonymous with all "white gardens". There are so many other white roses and perhaps 'Iceberg' is over-used, but it has proved to be a hardy floribunda with continuous flowering over a long period. It can be grafted as a standard and is also available as a vigorous climber – its versatility makes it a safe choice.

LEFT A wonderful bower of hardy roses climb over an arched metal arbour through which the restored La Ferriera can be glimpsed.

BELOW The sun filters through the gnarled olive trees which shade the natural stone terrace. Scented roses scramble through the branches, and others have been planted round their bases to provide a wonderfully sensual seating area.

Dan Pearson is possibly one of the most empathetic landscape designers practising today. His epithet "a sense of place" has made many garden designers take a closer look at our own work. Pearson is a self-confessed obsessive regarding plants and their habitat, and he has used his knowledge to great effect. Not shy of using unfashionable plants, he has flouted the modern trend to disregard roses, and has included them in previous commissions.

Violante Visconte and her husband Carlo Carracciolo purchased an estate near Latina, in southern Italy, the romantic-sounding Torrecchia. It was an abandoned medieval hilltop village boasting a ruined castle and granary,

Torrecchia, Italy

DAN PEARSON

begging to be restored to some of its former glory. Pearson was presented with a very strict brief from his clients. The garden had to be cool, with green and whites predominant and no silvers. It also had to be reminiscent of the nearby medieval ruined village of Ninfa, which had been undergoing its own transformation. And the regeneration had to be implemented quickly.

Pearson used the ruins as a natural climbing frame and planted the much-loved climbing rose, *Rosa* 'Madame Alfred Carrière' alongside white solanum,

Wisteria floribunda 'Alba', and bignonias to emphasize the beauty of the medieval walls. Reclaiming the gardens back from the wild was a mammoth task. They created new vistas, scrambled up steep escarpments to plant, lay an irrigation system, set a swimming pool within the castle ruins, and made shady terraces and tree lined avenues, all the while battling with the intense heat. Eight years on, a semblance of "order within disorder" has been brought about and the garden has now been given back its own sense of place. Sadly, Violante Visconte did not live to see the gardens mature, but both her husband Carlo and Pearson continue to work on it and carry out her wishes.

We only have to look to nature to see that there is a rose suitable for every inhospitable part of the garden. I have seen the most beautiful wild roses flowering in the driest spots, buffeted by salt-laden winds, and rooted in crevices and along roads with little soil or water, yet appearing to be perfectly at ease with their environment. We seem, however, to be reluctant to use roses in our

Difficult Areas

designs, even though there are numerous varieties, ranging from ramblers, fragrant albas, and damasks through to modern shrub roses that overcome the obstacles of shade, the sun-drenched border, sites exposed to polluted air, and the seaside. Although species roses adapt especially well to these conditions and suit modern garden design they are rarely used – perhaps because they only have one flowering period, depite being followed by wonderful hips. They are a beautiful resource and should be used more.

The white roses planted under the trees reflect back the light that has penetrated the canopy of branches, bringing luminosity to the garden.

I am always amazed at how keen gardeners overcome all odds to create a wonderful garden and make their own oasis. Rose enthusiasts seem to be some of the most determined gardeners. However impossible the conditions are, through intense sun, drought, windswept hills, or gardens collapsing into the sea, these doughty plantspeople are not beaten. They are spread across the world from New Zealand, where the climate is too wet for roses, to Italy, where the soil has to replenished frequently, through to Canada, where they have bred their own Explorer roses to survive the deep frosts.

The waterside can be a wonderfully calming place, whether it is a man-made pond or a natural lake, and there is a fascination that lures us to the water's edge. This is all the more intriguing when the area surrounding the pool has been planted up with deep borders filled with textures, colours, and fragrances. One of the problems is the dichotomy of using roses in conjunction with water. Many gardeners feel uncomfortable including a plant that is not usually associated with water; there is a growing number of designers and plant specialists who advocate that only plants that are native and in keeping with their situation should be used. Others do not hesitate to place a plant out of context, and are prepared to experiment and take the risk that the plant may not fit the criteria of the purist but, in the right setting, can make a wonderful statement.

In New Zealand, at Ayrlies, a lily pool surrounded by dense evergreens has been brought to life by a colourful mixed border brimming over with the prolific *Rosa* 'Ballerina'. This vigorous modern shrub rose, with small, single-blossom, pink flowers carried in hydrangea-like clusters, bloom over a long period of time. Mixed here with purple clematis, valerian, sweet Williams, and terracotta-coloured achilleas under the canopy of a silver-blue weeping cedar, it makes a strong statement in front of a dark and potentially dreary backdrop. This border has a long flowering season that will provide interest from spring, when the fresh rose foliage starts to appear right through to late autumn, when the last roses bloom.

In Suffolk, England, Tessa Hobbs has designed a rose garden to create a swathe of colour under a canopy of deciduous trees. This rose garden is also linked to a pond, but here the problem is not of enclosure but the absolute opposite, as the garden has an open vista through to the fields beyond. Here, lessons have been taken from traditional rose gardens by using a clipped box hedge to enclose a pathway and link the boundary hedge into the overall scheme. The roses, from deep pink through to white, have been planted up among water-loving plants that help anchor the design to the pond.

The seaside is a very hostile environment. Salt winds come straight off the ocean, and the lack of shelter means that only the hardiest of plants can survive.

OPPOSITE In Ayrlies, New Zealand, a deep pink rose clambers over the timber arbour at the pool's edge, while the lighter pink of *Rosa* 'Ballerina' has been used throughout to provide harmony within the border.

ABOVE In a garden in Suffolk, England, Tessa Hobbs has designed a decking path along the side of the pool to lead you through the rose garden on to a timber terrace overlooking the fields beyond. A white rose at the entrance of the path illuminates the way.

OVER PAGE At Martha's Vineyard, New England, USA, Edwina von Gal has cleverly used *Rosa* 'New Dawn' with its blush pink fragrant blooms to blanket a long trellis. This incredible corridor of flowers invites you down a gravel path to the sea and lighthouse in the distance.

These two factors combined with extreme weather conditions, from severe winters to summer heat waves, allow few shrubs to flourish. But the rose will do well. Look at the brave burnet rose (*Rosa pimpinellifolia*) which is found in shallow sand dunes and grassy sand hills throughout Britain, and is a visual delight in spring and early summer. Several roses can survive these harsh conditions including the rugosas and their hybrids, as well as some tough climbing varieties such as *Rosa* 'Compassion', *R.* Constance Spry, *R.* 'Madame Alfred Carrière', and *R.* 'New Dawn'.

Roses can be used to great effect in many inclement places. In my own garden I have a wonderful *R.* 'Albéric Barbier' clambering over a shady fence. I know that it is not the most perfect of flower shapes and is particularly prone to mildew, but it gives both me and my neighbour immense pleasure from when its first pale yellow buds appear very early in the season to its second flush of creamy-white flowers in early autumn.

In another dark corner of my garden I have *R.* 'Madame Alfred Carrière' scrambling up a white-stemmed Himalayan birch (*Betula utilis*), with its large, scented, loosely formed, white blooms arriving early in the season, adding a thrill to a dull patch. These roses are both hardy and vigorous once

established, and provide invaluable interest to what would otherwise be two rather uninspiring areas of the garden.

Rambling and climbing roses provide us with a great means of covering up unsightly features, buildings, or walls, or simply for softening a stark frontage without damaging the fabric of a house. For the best results, train them on wires and then prune and feed throughout the year.

Two garden designers, Arabella Lennox-Boyd at La Bandiera, Italy, and Annie Fisher, in California, have used climbing roses to great effect in their projects. Both houses are steeped in sunshine and have little rainfall; each is painted a warm colour wash. In both cases the solution has been to plant climbing roses, but, interestingly, the colours chosen are at opposite ends of the spectrum.

Lennox-Boyd has selected white roses, underplanted with grey-leaved, white-flowering perennials with the odd touch of yellow, and spiky agaves, which give a cool presence to the house. While in California, a bright pink rose, enclosed by a formally clipped, low, evergreen hedge, gives an intense glow in the evening sunlight. Both are powerful statements as to what should be planted in a hot climate, and both work well.

TOP LEFT In gardens of the Cellars-Hohenort Hotel in South Africa (*see pp.32–3*), roses have been planted in profusion, as they seem to flourish in the strong sunlight without being prone to pests and diseases.

BELOW LEFT At La Bandiera, in Italy, Arabella Lennox-Boyd has designed a cool border filled with soft-shaped, white-flowering perennials with blue-grey leaves and stiff-leaved agaves, and white climbing roses to match the shutters and complement the soft colour wash of the house.

BELOW In California, deep colour appears even more intense in the evening sunshine in Annie Fisher's formal design.

Our love affair with the rose has led gardeners to plant it in some of the most inhospitable climates. We expect it to thrive, flower prolifically, and shower us with a heady scent even though it has to struggle in extreme heat with little water. Roses have travelled throughout the world and in some areas flourished against all odds. Their versatility is outstanding, especially that of the new roses that have been bred to withstand heavy rains and bitterly cold winters, scorching sun and drought conditions, as well as a diversity of soils and conditions.

In sun drenched gardens the aim is often to achieve a Mediterranean-style garden, where the colours and plants transport us to a rosy vision of Italy or Spain. Here, colours are vibrant and there is a shimmer over the gardens. In these climates fragrant plants are unsurpassed as the sun's heat brings out their scent and makes one dizzy with desire. No wonder roses are among the favourites. Yet, many grow tall and spindly in such extreme conditions, struggling for water to support their blooms. They require a great deal of

Oakland, USA

BOB CLARKE

care and attention if they are to thrive in such intense heat. Nevertheless, whenever one travels to countries in this belt roses seem to be planted up every house, spilling over walls, and even growing in old oil cans – each one tenderly looked after by their proud owners.

In California roses are grown in abundance and to great effect. Here, two distinct styles of gardening seem to be surfacing. One, a subtle use of pastel shades in informal groups and mixed plantings, echoes a more traditional style found in England. The other makes you sit up and take notice; roses are used to spectacular effect, their vibrant colours mixing with Californian natives such as *Eschoscholzia californica*, poppies, architectural shrubs, and tropical perennials. The effect of combining these plants is colourful and very much in keeping with the heat and sunshine of California.

In North America many of the houses have wonderful wooden structures and arbours smothered in climbing and rambling roses. Nowhere can you see a better example of this style of planting than in Bob Clarke's garden in California. Constructed in terraces, it features seemingly solid pillars of roses, which appear to be supporting his pergola, and act as the anchor to the house to the ground below. His lavish mix of grasses, perennials, and low-growing alpines spilling over a low, red brick wall provides a dynamic tapestry of colour with this unusual combination of plants.

ABOVE *Rosa* 'Buff Beauty', with its fragrant, warm apricot-yellow, semi-double flowers, is a vigorous plant with a spreading habit. It is free flowering over a long period from mid-summer into early autumn. Introduced in 1939 in the hybrid musk group, it has become a firm favourite, as it is so versatile, good for hedging, and specimen and group planting.

RIGHT In the bright sunlight of Bob Clarke's Californian garden, the colours of the roses are not bleached out. Grown up the supporting pillars of the pergola, they provide a colourful backdrop to the planting below as well as a cool screen for the house.

Italy has a plethora of magnificent gardens, many steeped in tradition and some filled with glorious rose gardens, but few are contemporary in their design or execution. The garden of Landriana are amongst the most important gardens of the era following world War II. and their creator, one of the great gardeners of the 20th century.

In 1956 the Marquis Gallarati-Scotti and the Marchesa Lavinia Taverna purchased derelict farmland on the Latium coast near Ardea. The site was exposed to the winds blowing off the sea and had the added problem of mine and bomb clearance, a legacy from the Anzio landings in World War II. From this inauspicious beginning, the Marchesa undaunted began the creation of one of the most beautiful gardens in Italy, and in spite of the hot summers achieves a succession of colour and interest from spring to autumn.

The Giardini della Landriana, Italy

MARCHESA LAVINIA TAVERNA AND RUSSELL PAGE

ABOVE *Rosa moschata* 'Princess de Nassau' has a dubious background, but it was reintroduced by Graham Thomas in the 1970s. This late-flowering shrub rose, that repeats well into the autumn, bears musky, fragrant, semi-double, creamy-white petals with delightful golden stamens when in full bloom.

OPPOSITE At the Giardini della Landriana a profusion of white and shell-pink roses with golden stamens and glaucous leaves lead the eye to the grey-blue foliage of the olive trees beyond.

OVER PAGE The play of light on the silver leaves of the olive trees makes the contrast with the tree trunks even more dramatic. The restricted palette of hebes, silver-leaved pittosporum, and the massed grouping of one rose combine to make a sophisticated choice of plants.

The Marchesa started by planting around the property a shelter-belt of trees all grown from seeds donated by a family friend. Like many enthusiastic amateurs, the Marchesa placed new plantings without a grand plan in mind, and in 1967 Russell Page was invited to help with designing the gardens, giving them form and order. The landscape took shape and was divided into a series of geometric gardens linking into each other. Page's notes on Landriana recollect the Marchesa's incessant introductions of new plant materials collected from around the world and his attempts to integrate the plants in a harmonious way within his carefully calibrated designs. As the Marchesa's passion for plant propagation, experimentation, and new introductions grew, she ran out of room and frequently planted beyond the bounds of Page's initial designs. These then had to be adapted to a wider scale to take into account her numerous eclectic collections.

After many years of Page's counselling, the Marchesa came to understand his philosophy of restraint and proportion to bring about a sense of equilibrium, and make a harmonious whole. As a result, Page's design principles were reinstated, the thematic rooms with perfect proportions and sympathetic plantings began to reappear, and the gaudy, showy, exotic specimens removed. Order was restored. Deep borders planted under olive groves show off fine textures and subtle shades of grey, and plants spill over paths made of local Tufa stone, and typical Mediterranean plants such as cotton lavender (*Santolina*), rockrose (*Cistus*), and *Centaurea* are mixed with old-fashioned roses in long drifts. Early summer is a magical time, when the

LEFT In early summer the majority of the 500 rose species will be in bloom and the nightingales in full song. Many of the individual gardens contain swathes of roses but the most magnificent sight is the Valle delle Rose, which the Marchesa considered the most important of all the gardens.

RIGHT The informal planting of roses mingling with the mounds of shrubs anchored to the site by the tall cypress trees looks as though it has been naturalized.

soft, silvery-grey of the olives and native plants reflects light and produces a gentle look that contrasts with the stark shadows thrown by the intense sunlight. The grey-green monotones complemented by roses in pastel shades all help to conjure up a picture of cool pathways rather than walkways in the mid-day sun. This is a multi-layered combination that is both enticing and exciting.

The gardens are laid out on different levels cut into the hillside, culminating in a man-made lake with roses playing a major part in several of the 39 gardens. The long Viale Bianco is a stunning symphony in silver-grey foliage underplanted with massed, pink-flowering rose bushes set behind a border of *Pittosporum tenuifolium* 'Silver Queen' and *Hebe* 'Mrs Winder'. This creates a sheltered walk along a grey cobbled drive, where the sun filters through the branches creating delicate shadows on the paving, while in the distance are the cool, darker, clipped shapes of the Marchesa's beloved topiary. The formal Viale de Bonica is set along a stepped brick path intersected by corridors of clipped laurel contrasting with the informal white roses: *Rosa* 'Madame Alfred Carrière', *R.* 'Penelope', *R.* 'Sea Foam', and *R.* 'Sombreuil'. At one of the intersections, the Valle delle Rose follows winding paths along which there is an informal planting of *R.* 'Nevada' and *R.* 'Moschata' down to the lake. The roses have been allowed to reach their optimum size, and grown alongside *Elaeagnus* x *ebbingei* and soft grass paths, make a romantic perfumed setting leading to the water. Turn the other way at the intersection, and your senses are overwhelmed by the Valle delle *Rosa mutabilis*, where in a field this incredibly fragrant rose has been mass planted with *Pistacia lentiscus*, again drawing you towards the lake and plantings of zantedeschia and iris.

Landriana is a modern garden in every sense. It stimulates the senses and is a source of inspiration, a garden that has been reclaimed from an inclement environment but has been created from a great passion, yet with a sympathetic approach. It is a garden of dreams and ideas that can be translated into many gardens of today.

Jennifer Myers Garden, USA

JENNIFER AND FRED MYERS

Jennifer and Fred Myers are not afraid of using vibrant colour in their garden in Austin, Texas, or mixing traditional plants with those considered "modern architectural", at which purists would cringe. But Jennifer Myers is an artist who is motivated by using vivid colour combinations, and, where most people would step back and draw breath, she experiments. Her bold associations of plants and eclectic selection of materials, many picked up scrap, have been used to create a garden based on good classic design and have formed a delightful retreat. Nevertheless, she works within the constraints of the watering restrictions of Austin and only uses hardy plants that are drought tolerant and will survive the ravages of the Texas climate.

Jennifer Myers is passionate about art and the outdoors, and, being a visual person, she is able to balance and use complementary colours in the garden as she would in a painting. Her use of colour to unite the garden and house is exemplary. Bright splashes of cobalt blue draw the visitor through the garden, while a spot of vivid red of a 'Blaze' rose against a background of green explodes your senses. Another favourite combination is the pairing of *Rosa mutabilis*, with its flame-coloured buds that open to coppery-yellow single flowers, with a dramatic, peach-and-white-striped amaryllis. Green has been used to temper the blast of colour that assails you. Clipped *Ilex vomitoria* 'Will Fleming' provides structure, while lawns and mature trees surrounding the property bring a much-needed coolness to the garden, literally by providing shade and a sense of calm.

The garden is full of visual and sensory surprises, many of which are jokey and involve integrating junk shop treasures creatively with the plants. A rusted, antique, cast-iron fence has been planted up with roses, underplanted with

LEFT The informal, brightly coloured, cottage-style plants set in gravel in front of the giant architectural agave and dasylirion take you into the formal avenue of clipped holly, which in turn leads to the entrance of the house.

RIGHT Intensely coloured roses nestle in a crevice in the garden.

perennials and bulbs. Take the outside bedroom: it comprises an old bedstead framed by an old gate and rock walls, and although open to the elements is made warm and friendly with junk shop finds. The outdoor dining area is again colourful and welcoming with its Mexican tiled table and canopy of fairy lights. Rescued artefacts, timber, pieces of architectural reclamation, wrought-iron window boxes, and terracotta pots filled with plants adorn the Victorian house and terraces, giving them character and a sense of belonging to the garden.

Jennifer Myers' textural combinations are as interesting as her colour combinations; one example includes placing spiky agaves and succulents next to an old-fashioned grouping of roses, parsley, and achilleas. As an exercise in contrast she has old, pink-flowering roses 'Emily Gray' and 'Monsieur Tiller' mingling beside a massive silver-grey *Agave scabra*. In another section *Dasylirion wheeleri* has been placed next to *Rosa* 'Martha Gonzales' and old blush China roses. This would usually be an uncomfortable combination but here, in this serendipitous garden, it seems to work. The roses chosen for this garden are hardy and in favourable conditions will repeat flower continuously over a long period.

In fact the Myers' garden is a contemporary version of the 18th-century rococo garden. It is a walk through many contradictions and confusions that bring you up short but it is intimate with its rooms, full of ornamentation, asymmetry with a tremendous sense of fun, light, and decoration for its own sake and beauty.

BELOW Jennifer Myers replaced a thirsty strip of grass along the road with crushed granite planted with agaves and the old rose Gipsy Boy (syn. 'Zigeunerknabe'), with its cheerful cerise flowers that complement the blue-grey of the agave leaves.

OPPOSITE Planted in a pot on the back terrace is the bright red 'Blaze' rose, a *Rosa wichurana* hybrid, which climbs up the sun-drenched limestone wall in stark contrast to the cobalt blue of the painted door, reminiscent of primitive folk art combinations.

New York Roof Garden, USA

JENNIFER BARTLETT AND MADISON COX

Creative nightmares, roof gardens are fraught with problems. Inhospitable climate, high winds, weight constraints, air-conditioning units, local planning restrictions, residents' associations, the neighbours' requirements not to mention the threat of lawsuits, all make high-level gardens challenging. The inter-relationship between client and designer can also lead to a clash of temperaments. But here the collaboration of Jennifer Bartlett, the client with a split-level apartment set on several levels on a roof top in Greenwich Village and designer, Madison Cox, has been inspirational.

Cox's designs are influenced to a high degree by the Mogul gardens in Kashmir. Their combination of order and geometry, the divisions into intimate rooms and living spaces, together with the play of light and water, are to Cox sensual, pleasurable retreats into which to escape from the hurly-burly of daily living and from the intense heat. Following the original formal concept but incorporating softening influences suggested by his client, he created a series of garden rooms connected to the interior living spaces.

Lush planting, much of it set in formal clipped squares for structure, combines with the wilder inclusion of blush pink China roses, spilling over an arbour to provide essential shade, while in the strong sunlight, shrub roses flourish in deep containers. Elsewhere formality prevails, with parterres of boxwood and specimen conifers, cream-coloured stucco walls covered by wisteria and clematis, and a main axis with a contemporary wall-mounted fountain. All of these spaces form a "labyrinth of garden rooms, each half-hidden from the next to increase the fun of discovery".

Although through the years many of the plants have not survived the rigours of the New York weather and have been replaced with tougher specimens – the wind wreaks havoc on all roof gardens, the dozens of roses have thrived. Climbers are tied in for support and deep, galvanized steel planters are put in place to support their root system, along with a drip irrigation system. The garden is now an established oasis in Greenwich Village, and attracts a multitude of birds, ranging from hummingbirds to sparrows.

Here is a garden on many levels with a spiral staircase leading to the upper stages. The staircase and a catwalk are now covered by wisteria and 'New Dawn' climbing roses, which provide a sense of privacy, an essential ingredient for exposed town gardens.

Palos Verdes, USA

JOHN GREENLEE

The Palos Verdes Peninsula is only a 45-minute journey from Los Angeles, California. It benefits from a hospitable climate, which is cooled by westerly sea breezes that also flow over and around the peninsula keeping the city smog at bay, making this an idyllic place to live. However, coastal fogs can roll in off the sea and blanket the gardens close to the shore.

John Greenlee is a passionate plantsman with a huge knowledge of grasses, his first love, and roses, his second; he has an innate understanding of the ecology of a site. His enthusiasm is infectious, and his empathy for the right plant in the right location makes him a much sought after designer. Based in California, he was asked to take on a project in Rolling Hills, set in the highlands above Palos Verdes. His client, Patricia Johnson, an artist, had bought a house designed by the eminent Long Beach architect, Ed Killingsworth, whose work in the 1950s and 1960s was highly acclaimed. The house was originally commissioned by Ruth Shellhorn, a set designer working in the Los Angeles film industry.

The property sits on a ridge overlooking the Pacific Ocean at a 300m (1,000ft) elevation. just 1¹⁄₂ km (1 mile) back down the hill it would be in the fog belt, but here there is a perfect Mediterranean climate. Greenlee's client inherited a dated garden, with tired, traditional textural combinations of clipped hedges, junipers and other conifers, sycamores, and hybrid tea roses, but it did have stunning views. There was "not enough colour" in this typical mid-20th century garden.

Greenlee describes his work on this garden as "Mediterranean eclectic". He tore out the depressing conifers and ugly hybrid teas and created a series of "rooms", each one themed in yellows, pinks, and reds. Golden pampas grass is teamed with 'Mermaid', *Rosa banksiae*, and yellow kniphofia. It was essential to keep a check on the choice of plant material, or the integrity of the design would have been lost. He found the smell of the ocean exhilarating and related the plants to those growing there naturally. Roses in abundance were mixed with woody plants such as sage, and other natives found on the chaparral, and combined with Mediterranean-adapted species grasses. Greenlee believes that "roses and grasses make a fabulous combination, they are the thread that link all spaces in the garden", an opinion diametrically opposed to that of European-based Piet Oudolf. He found it rewarding working with an artist as her eye for colour was unsurpassed and she would often suggest adding a touch of bright colour. Greenlee admits that his client's ideas helped to bring an additional sparkle to the plant combinations.

ABOVE An exuberant mixture of small, white flowering roses with brightly coloured red hot pokers and salvias makes a colourful display, and is one that can survive the rigours of the Californian climate.

OPPOSITE A stone pathway winds down the hillside with stunning views across to the natural landscape. It is planted with a mass of carefully chosen roses, prostrate rosemary, shrubby convolvulus, and festuca grasses that flourish in this hot, dry environment.

Swimming pools are rarely at ease within their garden surroundings. Too many times little thought is applied to the imposition of this large structure onto the landscape. Not only are swimming pools frequently ugly and dominant but they are often tiled in the most obtrusive bright blues. They appear like huge gashes within a garden, with poor quality hard-landscaping dropped into the design and certainly very little thought about the planting set around the perimeter to integrate the pool into its setting.

A pool, by its nature, is a place for having fun. Space is needed for one to spend time relaxing and playing around the edges, so large areas have to be designated for pool houses, sun-loungers, tables, and umbrellas, as well as sufficient room provided to be able to play, chase, run around, and jump into the pool. Although contemporary pools have increasingly eco-friendly systems, most pools are full of chemicals and not very plant friendly, so the choice of plants is limited to a selection of hard-working varieties that can

The Krause Garden, USA
SYDNEY BAUMGARTNER

survive the traumas of being constantly splashed with chemical-laden water. To make matters worse, open-air swimming pools are normally built in hot, sunny countries, so that whatever is chosen to be planted in a pool border has to withstand constant high temperatures during the swimming season sometimes without the aid of an irrigation system. Finding suitable planting companions can therefore be problematic.

Fortunately, we can look to the USA and Australia for inspiration – countries that have been installing swimming pools since the early 1900s and appear to have developed an empathy for linking the pools with the surrounding environment. In the Krause Garden, in Santa Barbara, designed by Californian-based Sydney Baumgartner, the pool has successfully been cut into the sloping garden, with the wall acting not only as one of the edges to the pool but also as the retainer to an abundantly planted border.

The natural tree line provides height to the back of this pool and, with the second tier of white shrub roses and an under level of bright pink cascading over the wall down towards the pool, makes for an intimate yet dramatic setting for this simple pool. The clear blue sky with the high sun reflects the plants in the pool, making the border appear twice the size. The strength of this design lies in the simplicity of the colours used, and the restrained use of plant varieties.

Restricted, intimate areas are probably the most difficult to design. There are frequently many constraints and obstacles to overcome. With a small back garden there are usually numerous entrances and exits to tackle, as well as paths, gates, sheds, and mean little borders. Add to this the microclimate of an enclosed space and the frequent lack of light, with areas cast into shade

Small Spaces

by neighbouring buildings. It is fortunate if there is a warm wall or sheltered spot bathed in sunshine, because this is where something difficult can be grown. For me, rose growing in a limited space has always been a challenge and for that reason I always chose climbers as they require little room and add a vertical dimension to the garden. But many other rose lovers are not put off by these constraints and find space for shrub roses to be included within these limitations to great effect.

White roses trained over an arched gateway frame the view into the intimate space of a courtyard and house beyond. Using roses in this way is a clever means of guiding the eye towards a focal point.

Whether the garden is naturally small or it has been designed within a larger area to make a private, secret place, the design criteria are similar. It is essential to use plant material that is sympathetic to the space and will flourish in the chosen spot. If the garden is to be used as an extension to the house, an outside room, then uncluttered, honest linear designs are often the best solutions for small areas. Good architecture combined with quality landscaping materials and simple, understated planting schemes work the best. Otherwise, in a few years, if over planted, the garden will lose its soul, become over-crowded, turn into an unmanageable jungle, and have to be torn out and begun again.

Thomas Church was the greatest and perhaps first exponent of the garden as a continuation of the living space, where good design is foremost. Lawns were considered inappropriate and replaced by paving, and level changes were essential. If there is little room for manoeuvre, simple tricks such as adding a pergola to allow roses to scramble upwards and over add new dimensions to any garden. By creating these "virtual" walls we feel safe and enclosed. These structures entice people to enter, linger, and enjoy their surroundings. But there is also plenty of scope if the garden is for plants and not for entertaining. There is nothing more exciting than exploring a true plantsman's garden, no matter the size. The smallest plot can turn into a Garden of Eden, with the plants taking centre stage at the expense of a terrace or lawn.

BELOW LEFT *Rosa* 'City of York' trained over an ironwork arbour forms a stunning canopy in the centre of this garden. It is surrounded by a wonderful combination of richly coloured plants suitable for a small garden. A silver-leafed pear grows in the foreground.

BELOW A terrace enclosed by "pillars" of climbing roses and the fragrant evergreen climber *Trachelospermum jasminoides* creates an intimate shaded dining area within a much larger garden. This outdoor room is sheltered from prying eyes.

The Boardman Garden, New Zealand

KATHY BOARDMAN AND SERENA BLACKIE

The climate of Auckland is both a help and a hindrance to gardeners. Situated on an isthmus and near the Pacific islands with their tropical weather patterns, Auckland can experience every weather condition, all in the period of one day. Warm westerly winds in winter can be mild yet rainy. It can become cold but not enough for snow, and frost is a rare occurrence. Spring is a mixed blessing, ranging from calm and sunny through to stormy, hot, and wet, while summer is temperate with rain showers. This is not the best package for roses which are notorious for their poor tolerance of wet conditions. Nevertheless, they can be vigorous and do well in the heavier soils of the city. They are prone to all the usual rose diseases and predators, due to the humid summers but against these odds they can pay dividends with a flower display from late spring well into early winter.

New Zealand is home to many wonderful rose gardens, and the Nancy Steen Gardens in Auckland pay homage to a great rose lover and grower. There are also new gardens where the owner battles to create a modern rose garden. In her garden in in the city, Kathy Boardman, a mathematician, has designed an internal courtyard for her 1920s' Boston-style home. For her, symmetry and order are paramount – part of her very nature. Influenced by formal French gardens and the work of Russell Page, she was able to introduce symmetry through various axes in both her gardens and the house. Helped with the choice of appropriate plants by Serena Blackie, she was determined to plant roses, even at they were not suitable. Her choice of blocks of mass plantings of a few select varieties provides a sense of calm and order that Boardman feels is absent in the "cottage style". Roses number among her favourite plants and are not only found in her courtyard but throughout the garden, covering arches and used as standards to introduce a variation in height. Her courtyard doubles as "a playground for her three cats, Tom, Leopold, and Eleanor, safe yet outside", as well as being a restful space in which to relax after a hard day.

LEFT *Rosa* 'Iceberg', complemented by French lavender and purple-flowering pansies demonstrates in this contemporary parterre garden how traditional design can be brought right up to date to make a fragrant retreat in a small garden. The centrally placed fountain, reminiscent of the paradise gardens of the Mogul era, provides the musical sound of moving water, which is always pleasing on a hot summer's day.

RIGHT The raised platform covered by a rose-laden arbour at the end of a red-brick path makes a delightful focal point and perfect place in which to relax and soak in the heady perfumes of the roses and lavender. This is a garden of pastel colours and a restricted selection of plants, which combine to create a sense of calm in this busy age.

BELOW The dining-room terrace is surrounded by a border of mature shrubs and trees. Many roses have been introduced into the new planting, including *Rosa* 'Céline Forestier', *R.* 'Madame Alfred Carrière', and *R.* 'Penelope'.

BELOW RIGHT The view beyond the new glass windows shows the massed planting of ferns, hostas, and digitalis looking towards an original pear tree, which now supports the vigorous rambling rose 'Sander's White'.

OVER PAGE Contemporary architecture melds with traditional brick walls. The view through the extension shows the planting around the new pool, and *Rosa* 'Sander's White Rambler' scrambling up the trunk of the old pear tree.

Greenwich, England

DEL BUONO GAZERWITZ

When this Georgian house in London was restructured, the owners decided to add a contemporary extension – a happy blend of the old with materials of today. Once the renovation was complete, the garden had to be tackled. Landscape architects Del Buono Gazerwitz were brought in to simplify the garden in order to reflect the minimalist architecture of the extension. Their brief also stated that they had to keep as many of the mature plants as possible and retain the original character of the house and garden.

The garden itself was very established and contained many mature specimens, but it had become overgrown. This meant that the garden underwent a total, yet sympathetic redesign. The designers were determined not to lose the garden's special atmosphere. Their plan simplified the layout by introducing symmetry and a strong sense of linearity. They used reclaimed York stone and London Stock bricks to harmonize with the house fabric. The design is linked by two pools set at either end of the extension, with a wall of glass at one end and huge folding glass doors at the other – opening up a new aspect within the garden. Many of the original shrubs have been incorporated into the design, together with an abundance of roses, which perfectly reflect the character of the house and garden.

BELOW *Rosa* 'Altissima' is a repeat-flowering
modern climber that originated in France.
Its blood-red single flowers add an intense
splash of colour throughout the year and
are followed by large orange hips. It is a
favourite rose throughout the world but
does best in cool temperate climates.

OPPOSITE In the natural light of California,
deep bright colours look especially
impressive as they do not bleach out in the
sun. Keeyla Meadows has used harmonizing
colours in her own garden to create a lively
setting for a seating area amid the cottage-
style planting. An old-fashioned pink rose
climbs up the framework of her classic
timber house.

San Francisco is an exhilarating city with more than its fair share of talented artists and designers. It is always attracting the unusual and producing the unexpected. In Albany in San Francisco Bay Keeyla Meadows runs her design studio. She is an artist and a landscape designer, and her talents and design practice are legendary in the area. Her abstract garden sculptures are influenced by the work of Gaudí, Modigliani, and Picasso. Living close to the Bay means that there is a lot of moisture in the air; this softens the light, so her designs and choice of plants reflect her favourite Impressionists, Monet and Matisse, who worked with similar light tones.

The climate is not the kindest one to roses, which Meadows selects for fragrance as well as colour, as they are prone to rust and mildew and need sun for blooms. She has been known to pave areas and paint walls a brighter colour to attract more heat to encourage rose growth.

Meadows describes her work as informal, from cottage style to naturalistic and it carries her trademarks — colour, whether in splashes or all over, and carefully designed and placed artefacts. For her "when all the elements of

The Meadows Garden, USA

KEEYLA MEADOWS

the garden harmonize — plantings, furniture, sculpture, hardscape, containers, paths, and colours — it's paradise". Colour should be used as "vehicle for joy", and she does this to great effect. Her own garden gives the feeling that you are stepping into an Impressionist painting, where dazzling plants, foliage textures, and colours harmonize to make the whole picture.

Where other, more nervous, designers would suggest pastels, Meadows will use primaries. Nor does she shy away from setting strong colours next to each other. Her artist's instinct always match the tones and contrasts precisely. So *Rosa* 'Altissimo', with its intense blood-red flowers — rightly well loved in temperate climates — does not jar against against the pink washed clapboard but looks stunning in its glory. Her cottage style reflects that of an earlier era, full of the traditional plants found in grandma's garden, but there it stops. Due to the bright mix of colours there is nothing dated about her gardens, and the choice of roses within the mix brings out that warmth, cheerfulness, and texture lacking in many small gardens. Her gardens are the antithesis of the ever popular "white" gardens and, as such, are bubbling over with the joy of life. Her work is sometimes described as whimsical, and it is always colourful with hidden secrets and full of a vibrancy that cannot be ignored. It is little wonder that her eclectic style is in totally harmony with her less-than-traditional neighbourhood.

Palazzo Malipiero Barnabó, Italy

ANNA BARNABÓ

The mystery and romance of Venice is imbued in its very nature. Here is an ancient city that is teetering on the brink of ruin, in imminent danger of being reclaimed by the Adriatic on which it stands. Yet, it is teeming with life and has a colourful past. The canals with beautiful buildings lining their banks are the arteries, with bridges allowing people access from one side to another.

As you travel down the Grand Canal, a very special garden will come into sight. This is the small courtyard to the rear of the sober and imposing Palazzo Malipiero Barnabó. A sensual rose garden that is the antithesis of the stark architectural forms of the buildings that dominate it on its three land-based sides. The owner has based her garden concept on allegories of art and nature uniting in Venice, where a garden is considered to be an ornament attached to a building. This lush garden evokes the Venetian tradition to replicate patterns found in Oriental carpets, with its clipped box edgings, gravel paths, statues, a fountain, and the original Renaissance well set centrally. Geometry is foremost but is softened by the introduction of seductive roses in pastel shades which play a significant role in the mix, as the rose symbolizes woman in general and, more specifically, the Madonna. It represents love.

Venice is extremely hot during the height of summer but otherwise the heat is not too excessive although it does suffer from frequent thunderstorms and showers, hardly ideal for delicate rose petals. And to exacerbate the problems, as the buildings and gardens have been built on piles sunk into the seabed, erosion followed by the infiltration of salt water is a common problem. This is hardly a sound base on which to create a marvellous rose garden such as this.

The Palazzo opens out onto a paved courtyard and into the garden, which is guarded by 17th-century mythological statues. Love, care, and attention are lavished on the upkeep of the gardens. Earth has to be replenished frequently and the gravel paths that are constantly sinking have to be renewed regularly. The choice of roses was very important, each one picked for its flowering longevity as well as its colour and perfume. A mixture of historical (*Rosa* 'Fantin Latour'), modern (*R.* 'Peace'), ground cover (*R.* 'Snow Carpet'), climbing (*R.* 'New Dawn'), and trailing (*R.* 'Sea Foam') roses were chosen for their performance. They bring to the garden a sweetness and luminosity, and are in harmony with the high, mellow walls and the water. The garden provides a "dream-like serenity", and is an idyllic setting in which to escape the bustle of everyday life and take refuge from the inevitable fate that awaits this magical city.

OPPOSITE Traditional clipped box edgings with a grey gravel path set in a parterre pattern work extremely well within town gardens. Their simplicity and structure suit small sites, which are frequently surrounded by business clutter and mess from adjoining buildings. The paring back of all unnecessary detail shows the plants to their best advantage. They, as exemplified by this weeping standard rose, become the principal players on the stage.

ABOVE *Rosa* 'Félicité et Perpétue' is a non-repeat flowering Sempervirens climber that is a favourite for grafting onto stock to make standards. It has a naturally lax habit, which makes it easy to train. As it is so vigorous it requires regular pruning to keep its shape as a neat weeping standard.

It would be difficult to find a more evocative location for a rose garden. Set right on the banks of the Grand Canal in Venice, sheltered on three sides by old buildings, this parterre garden, with fountains playing and roses burgeoning with sumptuous flowers conjures up thoughts of another, perhaps more romantic era.

Pierre Bergé, the owner of this garden in Provence, loves gardens. He has two – one in Paris where he can retreat from the rush of everyday life, and this second one, a Provençal escape from city living. As a director of Yves Saint Laurent and a patron of the arts, Bergé has a keen eye for design and he channels this into his passion for gardens, although he believes that life in a garden is transitory. His garden designer, Michel Semini, lived a short drive away from the property, so his innate knowledge of the area, climate, and topography enabled him to create an outstanding garden within a few short months of being given the brief.

This is an elegant garden, divided into a series of intimate spaces, with courtyards linked together – each with its own unique quality and character, and dramatic wild gardens outside. In the smaller gardens the design relies heavily on textures created by the plant material, much of which comprises evergreens clipped into mounds or spires, or beautiful tortured shapes, where light plays with the outlines, casting shadows to bring drama into the mix. The courtyards are enclosed by either hedges or walls and make a

Pierre Bergé's Garden, France
MICHEL SEMINI

ABOVE 'Iceberg' roses are well loved by designers, and are probably the most planted of the white flowering roses as they offer a continuous succession of double, pure white, fragrant flowers well into winter in mild climates.

OPPOSITE The highly fragrant evergreen *Trachelospermum jasminoides*, with its tiny, star-shaped flowers, picks up the intensity of the massed planting of white roses on either side of the gravel path and leads through to the next courtyard, while enveloping the visitor with sweet sensuous scents.

significant contrast to the olive orchard that is filled with native wild flowers, and gives way to an air of freedom.

There is a selected choice of flowering plants, and each has been picked for its unique quality to provide a special atmosphere for the individual areas. The only garden where a mix of colours has been allowed is in the wild meadow, and this is liberating. The massive, clipped topiary, bun-shaped forms combined with the tall, finger-shaped cypress trees are punctuated throughout the season by colour highlights, such as the blue of iris in late winter and agapanthus and hibiscus in the summer months.

This garden style is highly reminiscent of the late Nicole de Vésian's Provençal garden, where architectural form is so important, and flowers are restricted to a few choice shrubs and trees. Nevertheless, this garden is stunning with its monotones, and none is more attractive than the white courtyard leading into the pool area, where a massed formal planting of 'Iceberg' roses and *Trachelospermum jasminoides* trained around a mellow, buff coloured stone arch make a perfect combination to assail the senses. The whole garden is filled with treasures found locally and placed to entice the visitor to take stock and pleasure in the surroundings. It is hard to believe that this garden is only 10 years old – it seems as though it has been in place from time immemorial.

Rose gardens are highly emotive and for years have been enticing us into their fragrant bowers by the appeal of their richly coloured blooms and perfumes. The rose's appeal is such that its oils have been used in toiletries since Egyptian times, its crystallized petals are eaten, and its scent used to mask unpleasant smells. Almost every town has its own form of public garden in

Public Places

which to display its prized roses. New rose collections and gardens are being installed every year across the world. In 2001, 3,000 David Austin roses were planted at Alnwick Castle, Northumberland, England, in a controversial and contemporary design. Apparently, our leanings are still towards more old-fashioned gardens. Perhaps one day this rose garden will be considered by the cognoscenti as one of the leading cutting-edge designs based around roses of this century.

This contemporary garden in Alpilles, Provence, is divided into two separate and disparate gardens. The Jardin de l'Alchimiste is in three parts – black, white, and red – which follow the work of alchemy and the search for the philosopher's stone; red and white roses are used to symbolize the transition of turning lead into gold. The gardens owned and inspired by Marie and Alain de Larouzière were designed by the Maurières Ossart partnership in 1995 from the derelict grounds of an old farmhouse.

Not all public gardens are dedicated to roses and frequently those that are can be found in the most unassuming places. Gantry Park, New York, is one such treasure. This very modern garden was reinstated on a disused brown site and has incredible views of Manhattan across the river. Hewn stone blocks and benches are placed throughout its small, well-designed gardens of mixed shrub roses. Gantry Park provides an open space where anyone at anytime can read a paper or play a game of chess. Unfortunately, my stay in this garden was fleeting, and I was only briefly able to take in its considerable charm, listen to the insect life buzzing in the flowers, and ponder on why the roses were flourishing in such a downtown spot, before rushing off to see my next garden. It is clear that this is a well-cared for and loved community garden that should be copied wherever possible.

Such free public gems are few and far between. In London we are spoilt for choice with our parks and green spaces, for we are well catered for in the Western world by a plethora of gardens open to the public for a relatively small price. Stately homes, châteaux, botanic gardens, private estates, and small residential properties all open their gates to us and allow us to explore to our hearts' content. They all offer an imaginative array of plants, some solely roses, and all we have to do is stand back and appreciate the hard work that has gone into creating these masterpieces.

To appreciate gardens in their context I recommend that you visit some of the places mentioned. I have already noted the recently created rose garden at Alnwick Castle (*see p.123*) in Northumberland, the seat of the Duke and

LEFT Newby Hall in Yorkshire is renowned for its herbaceous borders, immaculate clipped hedges protecting the "war of the roses" border, and its inspiring cornus with pink bracts that are perfectly matched by the magnificent roses bounding the path.

ABOVE Box-edged borders contain this superb wall of climbing roses underplanted by Madonna lilies in the Stellenberg Gardens, South Africa. As roses were not only European in origin, they have every right to bloom in an African context.

Duchess of Northumberland. The design was masterminded by the Belgium team of Jacques and Peter Wirtz and has stirred up a lot of controversy, but this is a new garden and it should be given the chance to settle in and for its roses to grow to their optimum beauty before judgement is cast. Look also at the beautiful gardens created by that master rose grower David Austin at Albrighton, central England. There are over 700 species in five different gardens, and all are magnificently planted and groomed to perfection. Here roses are planted informally and left to show their natural growth patterns against a backdrop of clipped, dark evergreen hedges. This is heady stuff and you will fill notebooks about roses that have caught your eye. It will set you wondering how to redesign your borders and plant roses in your own garden, and you will forget the care and attention required to create a garden of this stature. To stimulate the senses and cause even more confusion on the other side of the Channel, you will find Eléonore Cruse and Christian Biette in their inspirational garden at Roseraie de Berty (*see pp.68–71*). This haven of a naturalistic rose garden uses old rose species and from this has sprung a world-renowned rose nursery. The nursery and garden are open to the public during the month of June only.

In New Zealand, the late Nancy Steen, a great amateur rose collector, filled her gardens in Auckland with "old friends", which she went on to immortalize in her book *The Charm of Old Roses*. Today, she and her work are remembered in a garden commemorated to her name in the Dove-Meyer Robinson Park in Auckland. The Nancy Steen Garden opened in 1984 and includes 200 mainly old species roses, shrubs, and herbaceous perennials that Steen grew in her own garden, as she believed that "a mix of plants makes the border less formal and relaxed", and this garden follows her principles.

Another inspirational garden is found at Tresco Abbey Gardens in the Scilly Isles, off the southwest coast of England. Protected by the warm Gulf Stream Drift, this garden is filled with the most exotic plants collected by the Dorien-Smith family over many generations. It is a magical place to visit with the most unexpected collection of tropical plants, that reach great heights, and nestle against temperate natives and roses, thus making this an eclectic, yet awe-inspiring sight.

With garden festivals and flower shows now firmly part of the garden and plant lovers' calendar across the world, designers are allowed to spread their wings and try out new planting combinations and contemporary designs. Roses are to be seen in abundance, some looking very much at home in their environment, while others seem distinctly uncomfortable in their hostile surroundings. But these gardens and their use of rose material are not to be dismissed – there is a lot to understand about this new, harder, contemporary style that may well suit gardens of the future.

ABOVE A hardy but rather prickly rose that flourishes in hot climates, 'Louise Odier' is a beautiful old Bourbon. The sweetly scented, warm pink, cupped flowers entice the vistor to bury their nose deep into the open blooms. This non-stop flowerer benefits from being grown in the warmth of the sun.

OPPOSITE On the sunny slopes of Tresco Abbey Gardens, on the Scilly Isles, roses flourish under a canopy of exotics, while echiums and foxgloves flower in the exuberant, well-stocked borders.

It took a designer with a vivid imagination, spatial awareness, and lateral thinking to create the phenomenal gardens at Les Jardins de l'Imaginaire, Terrasson, in the Dordogne. And Kathryn Gustafson, the quietly spoken American landscape architect, is one such person. In 1992, alongside colleagues Anton James, Philippe Marchand, and Frank Neau, she won the commission to design a public garden "to encompass global and local garden archetypes while capturing the spirit of the place".

The 6ha (15 acre) park opened in 1996, and allowed the public to interact with a new style of landscaping and public planting. These gardens take in all of Gustafson's philosophies and trademarks: minimalism, dynamics, site sensitivity, and technological know-how. France is one of the few countries

Les Jardins de l'Imaginaire, France
KATHRYN GUSTAFSON

BELOW The contours of the land and the natural woodland beyond are linked by a sinuous rose garden, allowing visitors to walk under the broad, metal pergola and down the hill, while surrounded by a multitude of climbing and shrub roses.

RIGHT The galvanized metal framework supports a profusion of climbing roses, which create a suspended garden, while stone benches allow the visitor to sit and observe the full sensory experience at leisure.

that is prepared to invest in projects such as this – a contemporary garden inviting controversy. This is a risky business which requires huge financial backing, and many such modern schemes bring negative backlash from the critics and public alike. Such short-sightedness by those who "play safe" often brings to a halt imaginative schemes such as those designed by Gustafson.

The gardens in the park form a linked walk reminiscent of the 18th-century rococo gardens in England; one of them is a rose garden unlike any seen before. Set among the trees and following the land contours is a suspended framework of roses. A tall steel construction resembling scaffolding poles undulates along the hillside, creating a "bridge" between the wildflower meadow on one side and the natural woodland on the other. The area created beneath this impressive structure is a very public space, with mown lawn and benches set under showers of rose blooms to encourage visitors to linger.

The sight of all the climbing roses in flower is spectacular and the fragrance is overwhelming. The bright vibrant colours of deep reds, glowing yellows, and subtle pinks are in contrast with the other gardens in the scheme, where exuberant colour is almost non-existent.

This is an immense architectural structure, where members of the public can walk with ease beneath the floral canopy, while experiencing sensational scent. All Gustafson's schemes entice the visitor to be directly involved with the landscape. Not every one feels at one with her approach but many enjoy the experience. And everyone comes away with vivid memories of her extraordinary use of contemporary materials combined with traditional plants.

La Roseraie de l'Haÿ-les-Roses is the world's oldest existing garden devoted exclusively to roses. It is also a living museum where all kinds of ancient roses have been brought together and possibly saved from extinction. In 1894 Edouard André and Jules Gravereaux created a rose garden of breathtaking beauty and also of historical value. In 1968 its ownership passed to the municipality of Val de Marne, which has conscientiously continued the maintenance and collection of the roses.

The breathtakingly beautiful decorative rose garden lies at its heart. It is a formal garden with a central pavilion and flanking trellis arcades.

Roseraie de l'Haÿ, France

EDOUARD ANDRÉ AND JULES GRAVEREAUX

Its construction in 1910 coincided with the introduction of new rose varieties with exceptional blooms that could be "exhibited" in this area. Nevertheless, a stalwart, *Rosa* 'Alexander Girault', a rambler with vigorous yet graceful growth and reddish-pink blooms was needed to cover this large structure.

By way of contrast, yet in no way less dramatic, are the rose-smothered arches creating one of the most colourful pergolas in existence. For me they are too overpowering as all the senses are bombarded from every direction, which prevents the beauty of a single exquisite rose to be appreciated for its own sake.

BELOW In the ornate La Roseraie Decorative you can sit and absorb the intoxicating fragrance exuding from the massed planting of roses growing against trelliswork.

RIGHT Roseraie de l'Haÿ boasts one of the most magnificent and celebrated rose arbours. A truly romantic garden, and a very special tribute to roses.

The garden at Hyde Hall, Essex, was recently developed by the Royal Horticultural Society. Created by the Hall's original owners, Helen and Dick Robinson, it was donated to the society in 1993. It is set in flat, exposed countryside, and is frequently buffeted by the drying southwesterly winds in the summer months and chilling Siberian gales in winter, with an average annual rainfall of 60cm (24in). In less than 10 years, the RHS, taking on the challenge of taming this wild landscape, has created a series of gardens able to withstand tortuous weather, including drought. Many of the plants introduced by the Robinsons are still to be found here, although the old hybrid tea and floribunda rose garden ceased to flourish, and has been replaced by the completely new Modern Rose Garden.

Hyde Hall, England

ROBIN WILLIAMS SNR

There are two distinct rose gardens within the grounds, one a shrub-rose border filled with repeat-flowering, old-fashioned and modern shrub roses, which will delight the visitor with the palest pink through to the darker tones of rich purple blossom and heady scent. These are teamed with pale pink foxtail lilies (*Eremurus robustus*) and alliums, and over the years the garden will be planted with sun-loving shrubs and herbaceous plants to give a longer season of interest. All the plants in this border thrive in the well-drained, naturally stony, sunny site as they are protected by a tall conifer hedge.

Hyde Hall is no exception to the trials run by the RHS, and here rose training is a speciality. At the bottom of a hillside, two rope and post structures have been constructed and are now totally clothed in a series of rambling and climbing roses, most attractively pruned into a series of luxuriant curves smothered in blooms. Yet, it is the Modern Rose Garden designed by Robin Williams that provokes the greatest interest. Designed on traditional lines, with rectangular beds protected by box and yew edgings, it has been planted with a collection of roses whose colours reflect those of a nearby herbaceous border. These strong colours are refreshing in a country where a preference for pastels and white seems to predominate. The trial in this particular border is to show how to overcome the prevalent problem of replant disease. The whole of this garden, a previous rose garden, was excavated, with land drains replaced, and new topsoil imported prior to the new gardens being laid out. The roses are now thriving and when they are surrounded by mature hedges will make a cosy, colourful, contained are a within the main gardens.

OPPOSITE The Modern Rose Garden is currently exposed to winds that come rushing across the fields. In time it will be protected by hedging, which will also help the roses to prosper, although, the wonderful view will sadly be lost to the visitor.

ABOVE Rich colours of modern shrub roses have been chosen to reflect the deep tones of the herbaceous border, which is filled with the warm autumn colours of Michaelmus daisies, sedums, and feathery grass seedheads. This display of colour from the combination of roses and perennials will bring pleasure from spring through to late autumn.

Gilles Clément is a seductive landscape designer with a reputation for paring out unnecessary detail, leaving a simple structured landscape behind. He is famed for his project at Parc André Citroën, Paris, which he created in conjunction with landscape architect Alain Provost, and which is known for its distinctly contemporary minimalist design. Prior to this Clément worked on another public commission at the Abbey de Valloires in Picardy.

These gardens were created in 1989, and commemorate the pioneering work of the order of Cistercian monks from the Middle Ages onwards. The gardens set along a grand central vista emanate from the abbey, which was the

Les Jardins de Valloires, France

GILLES CLÉMENT

inspiration for the existing garden design. In the forefront of the abbey is a rose garden, and although formal in layout, and set around a Cistercian square, it is considered quite unorthodox as it mixes roses with medicinal herbs and decorative vegetables to link the gardens to the original work of the monks. Old roses such as *Rosa* 'Jacques Cartier', an exceptionally good repeat-flowering, double rose that does well in cold climates, have been planted with modern shrub roses, new introductions from the David Austin range, and two new roses bred to celebrate the restored gardens: *R.* 'Jardins des Valloires' and 'Rosa des Cistercians'. This is a fascinating series of gardens as some are strictly formal – which is fairly typical of French landscaping – while others are more informal, reflecting the "English style". Ground-breaking work is continuing on new gardens within the grounds and the most recent one opened in 2003.

LEFT A carpet of old and new roses
including *Rosa* 'Nevada', *R*. 'Marguerite
Hilling', and *R*. Eglantyne mixed with
perennials, culinary, and medicinal plants
create a link with the past and the work
of the monks. Two new roses, 'Jardins des

Valloires' and 'Rosa des Cistercians', have
been bred in recognition of the restoration
of the gardens and can be seen flowering in
the new rose borders.

ABOVE The grand central perspective runs
centrally from the abbey, which provided the

inspiration for the gardens, through the
rose garden set round a Cistercian square,
and then onwards to the enclosed garden
at the far end of the vista. This garden is a
mirror image of the abbey cloister set out
in clipped yew.

The gardens of Blois, France

GILLES CLÉMENT, ERIC OSSART, AND ARNOUD MAURIÈRES

In the town of Blois in the Loire Valley are two contemporary rose gardens, both with historic settings, and each one created by three of France's leading landscape design practices in a highly distinctive style.

At the Bishop's Palace, the partnership of Ossart Maurières created an enticing garden of carefully selected roses, each one chosen for its scent and repeat-flowering properties. Go to the upper terrace to fully appreciate the glory of the rich colours and pattern: a mix of whites, creams, and yellows, into pink and purple tones, until the tempo moves up a beat into warm oranges, yellows, and deep reds, underplanted with grasses and offset by copper beeches and ornamental crab apples. Almost hidden in the midst of the plants is a small pond surrounded by species and botanical roses. The 'Roseraie de Blois' was bred specially for the opening of this garden in 1991.

At the other end of town, a very different public rose garden was created by Gilles Clément under the walls of the Château de Blois. This design is more architectural. Conifer hedges are clipped into undulating shapes creating a pattern of waves interplanted with herbaceous plants, grasses, and *Rosa glauca* with its distinctive foliage, bright pink flowers, and prolific hips, and *R. mutabilis*, a rose that grows well in warm climates.

LEFT The rose garden near the château is laid out on a grid pattern based on a cross. The informal planting of herbaceous plants and roses is set between formal clipped hedges.

BELOW At the centre of the château's garden is a square seating area with modern benches. Massed roses behind the hedges introduce an airy feel above the dense evergreen.

The view from the upper terrace at the
Bishop's Palace in the town of Blois looks
down onto the rich rainbow colours of the
rose garden designed by Ossart Maurières,
with its ornamental crabapples and
copper beeches.

Wave Hill, USA

MARCO POLO STUFANO

Wave Hill, Riverdale, has one of the most spectacular vistas of any public garden. A few miles north of Manhattan, set high on a bluff overlooking the Hudson River towards the Pallisades, is an 11.5ha (28 acre) estate that is now one of the best-loved public gardens in New York state. Originally a private estate belonging to the rich and famous including the Roosevelts, Mark Twain, and Arturo Toscanini, until it was deeded to the city in 1960. Then the rot set in. The gardens quickly fell into neglect with the weeds choking the box and hybrid tea roses, and glasshouses falling into disrepair. Five years on, a non-profit-making corporation was formed to take on this sad and sorry garden. Its mission was to "study and demonstrate the interaction between people and the natural world". Two years later still, Marco Polo Stufano was appointed steward. His task was to bring life and beauty back into the gardens and woodlands of the estate.

Stufano, a graduate in art history who studied landscape architecture and horticulture, has a hands-on approach to his work. When he first saw Wave Hill he felt a deep attraction for it and a sense of place, that is still with him today. When lecturing on the restoration of these gardens, his pride and fervour are evident. The remaking of the gardens is still ongoing, and is very much a labour of love that requires team work and collaboration with other like-minded souls and investors.

Previous owners had planted collections of rare trees and shrubs, and these formed the foundation from which to work. Today, there are 18 small landscaped gardens, 10 woodland and wild areas, as well as historic buildings and greenhouses to maintain. The mantra throughout the year is "constant change" throughout the gardens.

The original formal rose garden was ripped out to make way for a much more approachable flower garden with the newly restored conservatory as its rear wall. This garden has been laid out with rustic fences, arbours, and pergolas to give support to climbers that catch the eye from midwinter to late autumn. The brick paths form the structure of the garden, while the mix of plants provide year-round interest. Roses play an important role in the dynamic, flowering during mid-spring through to early summer, along with peonies and dicentras. Roses are found throughout the gardens, trained over pergolas and bridges, and bring a splash of colour and fragrance as you walk by. The combination of *Rosa* 'Doctor W. Van Fleet', *R.* 'Sea Foam', an American favourite, and the deep pink *R.* 'Madame Grégoire Staechelin' is perfect for the informal cottage style of the flower garden and rustic timber work.

ABOVE On the wilder side of the garden, tall grasses mingle with self-seeded foxgloves, pale pink roses, and the architectural *Yucca gloriosa* and *Rhus typhina*, making an informal, naturalistic planting. There is a startling contrast of styles to be found in the Wave Hill estate.

RIGHT Climbing roses trained up wooden supports in the flower garden add to the cottage feel at the front of the restored glasshouse, which, in former days, was the formal hybrid rose garden. *Rosa* 'Sea Foam', a delicate shrub rose, is ideal for inclusion in a mixed border with delicate perennials.

Paeonia
'La Lorraine'
Lemoine, France 1901
Paeoniaceae

The Cranford Rose Garden, USA

HAROLD CAPARN AND MONTAGUE FREE

While listening to Stephen Scanniello, the noted rosarian, passionately describing his quest to search out long-lost species and rare old roses throughout the world, I realized that the Cranford Rose Garden was blessed with having such a passionate manager. This garden, inaugurated in 1928, encompasses approximately 0.4ha (1 acre) of land enclosed by a white lattice fence. The garden works were originally paid for by a donation from Walter Cranford and the initial 1,000 rose bushes were given by various nurseries. A further 2,000 roses were added in spring making 650 different varieties and species, and on its opening, the Cranford Rose Garden became one of the largest and finest rose gardens in the USA, and it is still treasured and highly regarded throughout the world.

Nevertheless, the constant maintenance and replenishment and addition to the roses took its toll on the garden, and in 1992 a soil-restoration programme was initiated. This was completed in 1996, and all the rare roses were saved and replanted. In the restored garden, the rose in all its many forms flourishes. In 15 rectangular beds that stretch down the centre of the garden the hybrid tea, polyantha, and floribunda collections are planted, as Scaniello feels that these varieties are best suited to the formal geometry. While roses with a more lax and informal habit are grown in the outside borders, where they are encouraged to scramble, ramble, and climb over the purpose-made trellis, posts, chains, arbours, and arches. The modern shrub roses introduced in the 1920s have later introductions added to them and have been placed back in their original locations. Low-growing and procumbent roses are allowed to spread naturally over banks, while climbers scramble in profusion over the pavilion. Today, the collection numbers approximately 5,000 rose bushes, accounting for 1,200 species and varieties.

The plan laid down by Harold Caparn was both formal and practical. The classical rectangular shape, set out in three long rows separated by wide bands of lawn, is enclosed by decorative trellis. The garden is edged with brick paths and lined with arches to allow climbers to cover the walkways, so that both visitors and roses alike can benefit from the layout.

Cranford is part of Brooklyn Botanic Garden, which is renowned for its educational programmes. Each rose is labelled with its name and date of introduction. Visitors are encouraged to study rose varieties to discover which ones are best suited to their particular region of the USA, and a series of booklets is available, advising which roses can withstand all kinds of pollution, climates, and maltreatment.

The Cranford Rose Garden is an inspiration for the visitor and professional. Flowers bloom from late spring until early winter, and during this time it is filled with colour and fragrance.

LEFT Rectangular beds planted with hybrid tea, floribunda, and polyantha roses run for 15m (49ft) centrally through the Cranford Rose Garden. Varieties of early modern roses have been replanted and are growing in their original 1928 locations, together with more recent introductions.

BELOW Climbing roses scramble up posts and over arches covering the pathway that runs around the garden. The borders are planted with old roses growing up cedar posts interspersed with wild species, while modern climbers and ramblers festoon the decorative trellis that encloses the garden, giving a long display of roses throughout the year.

There is a rose for every situation, whether to scramble over an eyesore or a pergola, to tumble down a slope or create a hedge or wild garden, as part of a border scheme, or in an exclusive rose garden. The appeal is obvious and can be seen in the beauty of the single, double, formal, or ragged flowers and the attractive ferny, glossy-green, glaucous foliage – the autumn

Directory of roses

hues are a plus. Some even have bizarre thorns but these are so attractive that it is worth growing them just for this alone. There are roses for all sizes of gardens, from the smallest spaces to the widest open areas. Some roses can grow in extreme climates and poor soils; they tolerate intense heat, deep freezes, severe drought, and torrential rain. To get the best results for any design, a little research can provide all the answers for the best selection of roses.

Acid yellow euphorbias contrast perfectly with the orange roses clustered around the dry-stone pyramid. The dark stems and newly emerging red foliage perfectly pick up the deep plum-red tones of the roses at the back of the border.

Rosa acicularis
Species
↕ 1.5m (5ft) ↔ 1m (3ft)
Hardiness zone: 3
A sweetly scented, rich pink species rose. Its single flowers have white centres, and the wiry thicket of stems is covered in small brown prickles. Grey-green leaves and good autumn colour. It survives the coldest parts of Alaska, Canada, Russia, and Scandinavia.

Rosa 'Adélaïde d'Orléans'
Sempervirens rambler
↕ 5m (16ft) ↔ 3m (10ft)
Hardiness zone: 6
A vigorous, old-fashioned rambler, introduced from France in 1826. It carries clusters of small, soft-pink to creamy-white flowers with a delicate primrose scent. Although it only flowers once, it does so for a long time. It is almost evergreen and is perfect for growing over arches, pergolas, and arbours.

Rosa 'Alba Semi-Plena'
Alba rose, old rose, shrub
↕ 2.5m (8ft) ↔ 1m (3ft)
Hardiness zone: 4
One of the oldest roses. Beautiful semi-double milk-white petals with dark yellow stamens are followed by orange

hips. The lemon-scented flowers appear in clusters and have one flowering season. It is easily trained sideways and, if pegged down, will break into leaf and flowers along the stalk. It needs the temperature to drop dramatically to flourish, as it must have a winter rest.

Rosa 'Albéric Barbier'
Wichurana rambler/grafted weeping standard
↕ 7m (23ft) ↔ 4m (13ft)
Hardiness zone: 7
A somewhat informal, semi-double, fragrant flower that opens from apricot-yellow buds into cream flowers that turn white with age. A vigorous rose that survives shady aspects and loves rambling up and over unsightly obstacles. It flowers in early summer with a second later crop.

Rosa 'Albertine'
Wichurana rambler
↕ 6m (20ft) ↔ 3m (10ft)
Hardiness zone: 7
A popular prolific flowering rambler that blooms once with occasional later flowerings. Very sweet smelling, coppery-pink, double and semi-double blooms. It is a reliable, healthy rose that survives neglect.

Rosa 'Altaica'
Species
↕ 2m (6½ft) ↔ 1m (3ft)
Hardiness zone: 4
This species rose has creamy clusters of single flowers with yellow stamens and a light and fruity scent. With a long flowering season followed by black hips, dainty leaves, and a slender upright habit, it makes a good choice for naturalized plantings.

Rosa 'Altissimo'
Modern climber
↕ 2.5m (8ft) ↔ 2m (6½ft)
Hardiness zone: 6
A good repeat-flowering climber with blood-red petals and golden stamens, followed by large orange hips. This vigorous healthy plant can also be grown as a shrub. It does best in cool temperate climates.

Rosa 'Andersonii'
Hybrid canina
↕ 2.5m (8ft) ↔ 2m (6½ft)
Hardiness zone: 5
This shrub resembles a dog rose with big, bright pink flowers with white centres and scallop-shaped petals. It is large and vigorous, so excellent for naturalized and woodland gardens.

Rosa 'Albéric Barbier'

Rosa 'Albertine'

Rosa 'Ballerina'

Rosa arvensis
Species shrub or climber
↕ 2m (6½ft) ↔ 4m (13ft)
Hardiness zone: 6
This is Shakespeare's original musk rose. It flowers once, bearing strongly scented, single, pure white blooms with golden stamens followed by red hips. Good for growing up trees and happy in the shade. Tolerant of poor soil conditions.

Rosa 'Ballerina'
Hybrid musk/shrub and standard
↕ 1.5m (5ft) ↔ 2M (6½ft)
Hardiness zone: 6
Introduced in 1937, this is a delightful dainty shrub with sprays of small blooms. It repeat flowers well into early winter. It can be trained as a short climber against a hot wall, but is better left to its natural devices as a specimen shrub.

Rosa banksiae
Species wall shrub
↕ 7m (23ft) ↔ 3m (10ft)
Hardiness zone: 7
A vigorous, almost thornless rose that is one of the earliest to flower. Its shoots are smothered with clusters of white or yellow, violet-scented, small flowers. It needs little attention, even in the driest and hottest positions. It can be used as

a boundary hedge between fields. There are several hybrids available including *R. b.* 'Lutea', a double-flowering variety.

Rosa 'Blanc Double de Coubert'
Rugosa hybrid
↕ 1.5m (5ft) ↔ 1.5m (5ft)
Hardiness zone: 4
A beautiful, pure white, semi-double rose with papery petals and an exceptionally powerful rich scent. Its strong and healthy habit make it ideal for growing in cold, wind-swept climates.

Rosa blanda
Species
↕ 2m (6½ft) ↔ 1.5m (5ft)
Hardiness zone: 5
A sweetly scented, semi-thornless, early flowerer. Rich pink flowers are followed by vermilion hips. Excellent for wild and naturalized gardens.

Rosa 'Blaze'
Modern climber
↕ 4m (13ft) ↔ 2.5m (8ft)
Hardiness zone: 5
Clusters of bright, dark red flowers are abundant in its first flowering, then followed by smaller shows later in the season. It is easy to grow, moderately vigorous, and relatively disease free.

Rosa 'Blush Damask'
Gallica-damask
↕ 2m (6½ft) ↔ 2m (6½ft)
Hardiness zone: 5
An ancient rose with dark and light pink, rather misshapen flowers with a sweet fragrance. It is an attractive shrub, but it only flowers once over a short period.

Rosa 'Bobbie James'
Multiflora rambler
↕ 5m (16ft) ↔ 3m (10ft)
Hardiness zone: 6
This small-flowering rambler has numerous white flowers followed by a mass of hips. Best when grown up a tree.

Rosa Bonica
Modern shrub and standard
↕ 1.5m (5ft) ↔ 1.5m (5ft)
Hardiness zone: 5
A repeat-flowering, sweetly scented, relatively disease-free rose. Its spreading habit makes it good for groundcover, and it can be grown in containers.

Rosa 'Boule de Neige'
Noisette
↕ 1.5m (5ft) ↔ 1m (3ft)
Hardiness zone: 6
This repeat-flowering old rose has richly fragrant, white blooms, which are full

Rosa Bonica

Rosa 'Boule de Neige'

then turn into the classic "cabbage" shape. It does not tolerate rain well and although hardy, needs a hot climate to achieve its full potential.

Rosa 'Buff Beauty'
Musk
↕ 2m (6½ft) ↔ 1.5m (5ft)
Hardiness zone: 6
The tea rose-shaped flowers appear in large trusses, and vary in colour from apricot-yellow to a rich buff. It has a lax habit and can be trained up a wall in hot climates. In cooler climates and shade it keeps its colour, and flowers into winter.

Rosa californica
Species
↕ 2m (6½ft) ↔ 1.5m (5ft)
Hardiness zone: 6
A robust species rose that can withstand severe drought and cold. Small rose-pink flowers with little red hips. It needs a lot of space and is ideal for naturalizing.

Rosa canina
Species
↕ 4m (13ft) ↔ 3m (10ft)
Hardiness zone: 5
The dog rose found widely throughout the world with its distinctive pink petals with white centres has a short-lived

flowering spell and is followed by bright red hips. Too large for a garden plant but ideal for a naturalized planting.

Rosa 'Cantabrigiensis'
Species
↕ 2m (6½ft) ↔ 2m (6½ft)
Hardiness zone: 5
Clear, light yellow, single flowers with a delicate perfume. It makes a dense shrub. Good for early colour in the border and in naturalized gardens.

Rosa 'Captain Samuel Holland'
Explorer x kordesii climber
↕ 2m (6½ft) ↔ 1m (3ft)
Hardiness zone: 3
A hardy 1991 introduction named after George III's surveyor-general in Canada. Its crimson-red flowers are flat and lightly scented. Relatively disease free and repeats very well.

Rosa 'Cécile Brünner' syn.
R. 'Madame Cécile Brunner'
Polyantha shrub and climber
↕ 1–6m (3–20ft) ↔ 1–3m (3–10ft)
Hardiness zone: 6
Masses of tiny, tea rose-shaped, very fragrant, blush-pink flowers. It is repeat flowering. This vigorous shrub requires little pruning and is easy to grow.

Rosa centifolia (Cabbage Rose)
Centifolia shrub
↕ 1.5m (5ft) ↔ 1.5m (5ft)
Hardiness zone: 4
A rose, often featured in old Dutch masterpieces, with a strong fragrance and beautiful, globular pale pink flowers. A lax habit gives an open shrub. A vigorous, healthy plant.

Rosa 'Charles Austin'
English shrub
↕ 2m (6½ft) ↔ 1.2m (4ft)
Hardiness zone: 5
An early David Austen introduction named after his father. A warm apricot-coloured rose with a fruity fragrance. It repeats well through a long season, but only if it is pruned back after the first flowering. In a warm climate, planted against a wall, it can reach 3m (10ft). A little prone to blackspot and mildew.

Rosa 'Charles Rennie Mackintosh'
English shrub
↕ 1m (3ft) ↔ 80cm(32in)
Hardiness zone: 5
A small, compact, disease-resistant rose with a musky fragrance from the David Austin stable. Its flowers are an unusual, soft lilac-pink colour. It repeats well and tolerates rain and hot, dry summers.

Rosa 'Buff Beauty'

Rosa centifolia

Rosa 'Compassion'
Modern climber
↕ 3m (10ft) ↔ 2m (6½ft)
Hardiness zone: 6

Salmon-pink tinted, apricot-orange, hybrid tea-shaped, richly scented flowers. A vigorous climber that repeats well.

Rosa 'Constance Spry'
English shrub and climber
↕ 2.5m (8ft) ↔ 1.5m (5ft)
Hardiness zone: 6

An early David Austin introduction. The superb clear pink flowers have a strong myrrh fragrance. It blooms once and looks its best when tied in as a climber.

Rosa 'Danse du Feu' syn.
R. 'Spectacular'
Modern climber
↕ 3m (10ft) ↔ 2m (6½ft)
Hardiness zone: 5

A continuous-flowering, vigorous climber with semi-double blooms. It gives a good contrast between the vivid red flowers and the dark green foliage. An excellent choice for a red climber.

Rosa 'Desprez à Fleurs Jaunes'
Noisette climber
↕ 5m (16ft) ↔ 3m (10ft)
Hardiness zone: 7

Old-fashioned, flat, warm yellow shaded peach flowers with a rich fragrance. It is easy to grow in hot climates, but prone to disease in cool, wet weather.

Rosa 'Dublin Bay'
Modern climber
↕ 3m (10ft) ↔ 2m (6½ft)
Hardiness zone: 5

A good rose for training up pillars or trellis, against a wall, or as a hedge. Strong in growth and intense in colour. This repeat flowerer has bright crimson flowers and dark foliage. It is tolerant of heat and cold. Good disease resistance and a very long flowering season.

Rosa 'Emily Gray'
Wichurana rambler/
weeping standard
↕ 5m (16ft) ↔ 2m (6½ft)
Hardiness zone: 7

Beautiful, fragrant, golden-yellow flowers are carried on healthy growth. It requires little pruning when young and in later years is covered in blooms.

Rosa 'Félicité et Perpétué'
Sempervirens hybrid/climber and weeping standard
↕ 5m (16ft) ↔ 3m (10ft)
Hardiness zone: 5

Large clusters of pompom-shaped, creamy-white, tinged with pink blooms smother a dense mass of growth. Exudes a strong musk fragrance. Its lax habit makes it easier to train over arches and into trees.

Rosa 'Fountain' syn. R. 'Fontaine',
R. 'Red Prince'
Modern shrub
↕ 2m (6½ft) ↔ 1.2m (4ft)
Hardiness zone: 6

This rose has a heady scent. Its semi-double, blood-red flowers resemble those of a large floribunda. An exceptionally strong and hardy shrub, which looks good as a bedding rose.

Rosa gallica
Species
↕ 1m (3ft) ↔ 1m (3ft)
Hardiness zone: 5

An important species rose as its genes are to be found in the majority of modern roses. It grows to a small bush in the wild, but reaches a larger size in cultivation. The blooms are made up of delightful, bright pink petals with a white eye and prominent golden stamens. It has a good fragrance. *R. g.* 'Versicolor' has reddish-pink blooms striped pale pink.

Rosa 'Compassion'

Rosa 'Constance Spry'

Rosa 'Fountain'

Rosa 'Galway Bay'
Modern cllimber
↕ 3m (10ft) ↔ 2.5m (8ft)
Hardiness zone: 6
A good, repeat-flowering, fragrant climber with salmon-pink blooms. A hardy plant that is almost continuously in flower throughout the summer.

Rosa 'Geranium'
Species/large shrub and climber
↕ 4m (13ft) ↔ 4m (13ft)
Hardiness zone: 5
With brilliant red flowers and yellow stamens followed by large, pendulous, scarlet hips, this species rose makes a good splash of colour in a border or in the naturalized garden. It grows into a tall, arching bush, and makes a good autumn feature.

Rosa 'Gipsy Boy'
syn. *R.* 'Zigeunerknabe'
Shrub rose
↕ 1.5m (5ft) ↔ 2m (6½ft)
Hardiness zone: 4
Related to Gallica roses, it has a series of small, dark purple-crimson petals laid out in neat circles around a centre of golden stamens. This vigorous shrub is highly scented, although susceptible to blackspot.

Rosa glauca syn. *R. rubrifolia*
Species
↕ 2m (6½ft) ↔ 1.5m (5ft)
Hardiness zone: 4
A rose for all borders and naturalized plantings with its plum-grey foliage, and delightful, small, carmine flowers with white centres followed by red hips. Hardy in cold climates but does not flourish in hot, sun drenched weather.

Rosa 'Gloire de Dijon'
Climbing tea
↕ 5m (16ft) ↔ 3m (10ft)
Hardiness zone: 6
A strong, repeat-flowering rose with buff-yellow petals and good fragrance. An old tea rose dating back to 1853.

Rosa 'Golden Showers'
Modern climber
↕ 4m (13ft) ↔ 5m (16ft)
Hardiness zone: 7
An early, repeat-flowering climber which thrives in mild climates. It has sweetly scented, golden-yellow flowers. Tolerant of rain and shade in hot climates.

Rosa 'Golden Wings'
Modern shrub
↕ 2m (6½ft) ↔ 1.5m (5ft)
Hardiness zone: 5

This hardy shrub with its almost single, pale yellow, fragrant flowers with mahogany coloured stamens can withstand wind and rain. If left unpruned, it has orange hips, which make a good display well into winter.

Rosa 'Gruss an Aachen'
Floribunda
↕ 80cm (32IN) ↔ 80cm (32IN)
Hardiness zone: 6
This delightful, compact, spreading rose with lightly fragrant, double blooms, flesh pink aging to cream, repeats well. Moderately vigorous, it responds well to watering and feeding.

Rosa hugonis
Species shrub and standard
↕ 2m (6½ft) ↔ 2.5M (8ft)
Hardiness zone: 5
A healthy, vigorous rose and one of the earliest to bloom in spring when its delicate, primrose-yellow, single flowers smother the ferny leafed branches. Good autumn colour with crimson leaves and red hips.

Rosa 'Ispahan'
Damask
↕ 2m (6½ft) ↔ 2m (6½ft)
Hardiness zone: 5

Rosa 'Gipsy Boy'

Rosa glauca

Rosa 'Gruss an Aachen'

A semi-evergreen old rose with deliciously scented, mid pink flowers. Its one flowering lasts over a long period.

Rosa 'Jacqueline du Pré'
Modern shrub
↕ 1.5m (5ft) ↔ 1.2m (4ft)
Hardiness zone: 6
Related to the Scottish roses, this semi-double, blush-pink rose is a hardy, vigorous shrub. It blooms early, repeats well, and has a light, musky scent.

Rosa 'Jens Munk'
Explorer x rugosa
↕ 1.2m (4ft) ↔ 1.2m (4ft)
Hardiness zone: 3
An incredibly hardy rose that will survive the most severe winters but also thrive in hot climates. A repeat-flowering, sweetly scented, semi-double, rich pink flower on a relatively disease-free plant.

Rosa 'Kiftsgate'
Species rambler
↕ 10m (33ft) ↔ 4m (13ft)
Hardiness zone: 6
Small, single, highly fragrant, white flowers followed by a multitude of tiny orange hips. A very vigorous rambler, only for large gardens. Excellent for training up trees or over buildings.

Rosa 'La Reine'
Hybrid perpetual
↕ 1.8m (6ft) ↔ 1.5m (5ft)
Hardiness zone: 5
Introduced in 1842 and still highly regarded as a repeat-flowering, strongly scented, dark lilac-pink rose. It produces few thorns and long stems, which can be pegged to the ground to increase their flowering.

Rosa laevigata (Cherokee rose)
Species shrub or rambler
↕ 5m (16ft) ↔ 5m (16ft)
Hardiness zone: 7
Its shiny evergreen foliage is the perfect foil for the large, solitary, white, sweetly fragrant, late-spring flowers with golden stamens. Bright orange, bristly hips appear in autumn. Very hardy in tropical lowlands, but in cold areas it needs the shelter of a warm wall.

Rosa 'Leverkusen'
Kordesii climber/weeping standard
↕ 3m (10ft) ↔ 2m (6½ft)
Hardiness zone: 4
Large, double, fragrant, pale yellow blooms held in clusters, which are constantly in flower until late in the season. Strong and healthy with hips that turn yellow very late in the year.

Rosa 'Marguerite Hilling'
Modern shrub
↕ 3m (10ft) ↔ 4m (13ft)
Hardiness zone: 4
Hardy from cold northern to hot southern climates, this sport of 'Nevada', after a period of settling in, grows into a large specimen with sweet-smelling pink blooms covering the bush.

Rosa 'Martha's Vineyard'
Modern shrub
↕ 75cm (30in) ↔ 1.5m (5ft)
Hardiness zone: 5
A healthy introduction from Denmark. Tolerates extremes of heat and cold. Clusters of semi-double, bright crimson roses with a white centre when they open out. Continuously flowers throughout the season. Low and wide in habit, it makes an excellent hedge.

Rosa Mary Rose
Modern english shrub/standard
↕ 1.2m (4ft) ↔ 1.2m (4ft)
Hardiness zone: 5
Clusters of sweetly scented, cup-shaped, loosely double, rose-pink blooms. It is named after Henry VIII's flagship that was recovered after 400 years. A good, continuous-flowering, disease-resistant shrub for mixed borders.

Rosa 'Marguerite Hilling'

Rosa Mary Rose

Rosa 'Mermaid'
Bracteata climber
↕ 5m (16ft) ↔ 4m (13ft)
Hardiness zone: 6
Slow to establish, with vicious barbs, but worth the wait and pain. Resents pruning, but produces the most wonderful, sulphur-yellow, large, single flowers continuously over a long season. If left it will eventually grow into a very large plant.

Rosa 'Minnehaha'
Wichurana rambler
↕ 4m (13ft) ↔ 2m (6½ft)
Hardiness zone: 5
A rampant rambler with a multitude of elegant pink sprays of lightly scented blooms. Requires little pruning and, if left, can grow into a huge thicket covered in flowers. It does well in Mediterranean climates.

Rosa 'Madame Alfred Carrière'
Noisette climber
↕ 5m (16ft) ↔ 2m (6½ft)
Hardiness zone: 7
A reliable and hardy old rose that rewards with the continuous flowering of large, sweetly scented, white blooms tinted with flesh pink over a long period. It is disease resistant.

Rosa 'Madame Grégoire Staechelin'
syn. R. 'Spanish Beauty'
Modern climber
↕ 4m (13ft) ↔ 2.5m (8ft)
Hardiness zone: 6
A magnificent climber carrying masses of clear pink flowers early in the season in temperate regions. Its strong fragrance is similar to the scent of sweet peas. This vigorous and reliable climber gives a showy display.

Rosa 'Madame Isaac Pereire'
Bourbon shrub/small climber
↕ 2.5m (8ft) ↔ 2m (6½ft)
Hardiness zone: 6
Old-fashioned, large, fragrant, cup-shaped blooms in a deep pink. A repeat flowerer that looks good in a mixed border with silvers, greys, blues, and purple. It can be pegged to the ground to encourage new growth and flowers.

Rosa moyesii
Species shrub
↕ 4m (13ft) ↔ 4m (13ft)
Hardiness zone: 5
An impressive species rose with dark green foliage, vivid blood-red flowers, and large crimson hips. Its open habit of arching stems makes it suitable for large gardens, and it is ideal for wild woodland and naturalistic plantings.

Rosa mutabilis
China rose
↕ 2m (6½ft) ↔ 2.5m (8ft)
Hardiness zone: 7
In warm, sheltered conditions it flowers continuously. Its petals change colour, starting with flame coloured buds through copper-yellow, and, with age, turning pink and coppery-crimson.

Rosa 'Nevada'
Modern shrub
↕ 3m (10ft) ↔ 4m (13ft)
Hardiness zone: 4
The added delight of this shrub rose is the reddy-brown colour of the stems, which support a mass of large creamy-white blooms along its branches. One of the earliest in flower, it continues intermittently through a long season. Very hardy from cold to hot regions.

Rosa 'New Dawn'
Wichurana rambler
↕ 4m (13ft) ↔ 2m (6½ft)
Hardiness zone: 5
In 1997 it was awarded the coveted title "World's Favourite Rose" by the World Rose Federation in America. Its silvery

Rosa 'Madame Alfred Carrière'

Rosa moyesii

Rosa mutabilis

blush-pink flowers are carried in clusters, and in clement climates it flowers until winter. A vigorous and hardy rose with a fruity fragrance.

Rosa nitida

Species

↕ 80cm (32in) ↔ 80cm (32in)

Hardiness zone: 4

This small, rugged species rose is found naturally growing in eastern Canada and New England, USA. Deep bright pink flowers are followed by bristly vermilion hips. In autumn its leaves turn attractive shades of red, orange, and yellow.

Rosa 'Nuits de Young'

Moss

↕ 1.5m (5ft) ↔ 1m (3ft)

Hardiness zone: 4

The unique colour, a dark dusky purple, and its strong, sweet fragrance make this otherwise sparsely leaved old rose a jewel in the border. Suitable for small spaces and tolerant of poor soil.

Rosa officinalis syn. R. 'Red Rose of Lancashire', R. 'Apothecary's Rose'

Gallica

↕ 1.2m (4ft) ↔ 1.2m (4ft)

Hardiness zone: 5

A wonderful ancient variety with a strong heady scent and large, semi-double, crimson flowers. Only flowers once but then in such profusion it is worthy of being included in a rose garden, parterre, or border. Extremely tough, healthy, and reliable.

Rosa 'Old Blush' (the Monthly rose)

China

↕ 1m (3ft) ↔ 1m (3ft)

Hardiness zone: 6

One of the first roses to flower and it will continue through to mid-winter. This "last rose of summer" has delicate pale pink blooms held in clusters with a deliciously strong fragrance.

Rosa 'Omar Khayyám'

Damask

↕ 2m (6½ft) ↔ 2m (6½ft)

Hardiness zone: 5

Small, pale pink, fragrant flowers named after the Persian poet Omar Khayyám, famous in the 19th century. It is said that seeds from hips brought back from a rose on the poet's grave were cultivated into this rose. An interesting variety because of its history rather than its blooms, but worthy of inclusion in an "historical" rose garden.

Rosa 'Ophelia'

Hybrid tea/shrub and climber

↕ 1m (3ft) ↔ 80cm (32in)

Hardiness zone: 6

Rich, flesh pink flowers from classic tea rose buds. Unlike many later hybrid tea introductions, it has a rich, sweet fragrance and good foliage. It repeats well over a long season. It is credited with about 30 sports and was the industry standard for hybrid teas.

Rosa 'Papillon'

China tea

↕ 1.5m (5ft) ↔ 1m (3ft)

Hardiness zone: 7

This little known China rose has delightful, double, ragged petals, which are predominately pink with soft overtones of copper from the base. It has a light, sweet scent and reliable repeat flowering. Usually grown as a bush but it can also be trained up pillars. Tolerant of hot conditions.

Rosa 'Parkdirektor Riggers'

Kordesii climber

↕ 4m (13ft) ↔ 2m (6½ft)

Hardiness zone: 4

A German introduction in 1957 with good repeat flowering. The clusters of deep glossy, crimson flowers against

Rosa 'Nevada'

Rosa 'Old Blush'

dark green leaves look better if grown in bright sunshine. It is tolerant of extremes of temperature, so makes a good red climber in problem gardens.

Rosa 'Paul's Himalayan Musk'
Musk rambler

↕ 5m (16ft) ↔ 3m (10ft)
Hardiness zone: 6

Planted at the base of a tall tree, this rambler can scramble to the top and give a wonderful display of small, blush-pink flowers with a heady perfume. One of the best ramblers, vigorous and hardy in unpromising situations.

Rosa 'Paul's Lemon Pillar'
Tea noisette

↕ 3.5m (11ft) ↔ 2m (6½ft)
Hardiness zone: 7

The large, waxy, creamy-lemon, highly fragrant flowers are green tinged in the centres. It flowers once only, but it is hardy and vigorous in hot, dry climates. Avoid growing in rainy areas.

Rosa 'Peace' syn. *R.* 'Madame A. Meilland', *R.* 'Gioia', *R.* 'Gloria Dei'
Hybrid tea/shrub and climber

↕ 1.5m (5ft) ↔ 1.2m (4ft)
Hardiness zone: 6

Possibly the most renowned rose across the English-speaking world, it has elegant buds, which open into huge flowers with a rich fruity fragrance. The petals are very soft yellow with a crimson edge, which pales to cream and pink. It grows best in cool climates.

Rosa 'Penelope'
Hybrid musk

↕ 2m (6½ft) ↔ 2m (6½ft)
Hardiness zone: 7

A very hardy, repeat-flowering rose with a sweet musky fragrance. It bears large trusses of creamy-pink blooms. Tolerant of poor soils and shade, it grows well in both cool and hot climates.

Rosa pimpinellifolia
syn. *R. spinosissima* (Scotch rose, Burnet rose)
Species

↕ 1m (3ft) ↔ 1m (3ft)
Hardiness zone: 4

An ideal groundcovering rose, as it is low growing and covered in a profusion of small, white flowers in late spring and again in early summer, followed by small black hips. It is good for growing on poor soils. A native of Europe, living in habitats ranging from mountains to the seaside.

Rosa 'Rambling Rector' ('Seagull')
Multiflora rambler

↕ 3.5m (11ft) ↔ 2m (6½ft)
Hardiness zone: 6

This hardy Irish introduction has a delicious fragrance and a mass of small, creamy-white, semi-double flowers that smother the vigorous stems as they clamber up trees or over pergolas. Orange hips appear in autumn.

Rosa 'Roseraie de l'Haÿ'
Rugosa

↕ 17m (56ft) ↔ 2m (6½ft)
Hardiness zone: 4

A fine rugosa hybrid with rich purple-wine coloured buds, which open into crimson-purple fragrant blooms on vigorous dense shrubs. Stems are covered with spines and light green foliage, which turns into glorious autumn tones.

Rosa rugosa
Species

↕ 1.2 (4ft) ↔ 1.5m (5ft)
Hardiness zone: 3

A naturally repeat-flowering wild rose. Its variable purple-rose coloured blooms are very fragrant. It is frequently used as a hedging plant. Tolerant of extreme conditions including sand, so can be used to stabilize coastal dunes.

Rosa 'Penelope'

Rosa pimpinellifolia

Rosa rugosa

Rosa 'Sally Holmes'
Modern shrub/climber
↕ 1.5m (5ft) ↔ 2m (6½ft)
Hardiness zone: 5
A good continuous-flowering small
shrub with clusters of cream tinged
with pink blossoms that smother the
branches. Tolerant of rain and hot
conditions, but it needs supporting in
windy conditions. A hardy, relatively
disease-resistant rose.

Rosa 'Sarah van Fleet'
Rugosa
↕ 2m (6½ft) ↔ 1.5m (5ft)
Hardiness zone: 4
Semi-double, mallow-pink, highly
scented flowers that repeat well.
A very hardy, weather resistant, reliable
hybrid suitable for hot climates.

Rosa 'Schoolgirl'
Modern climber
↕ 3.5m (11ft) ↔ 2m (6½ft)
Hardiness zone: 6
A good repeat-flowering rose. Its
fragrant double blooms in a delightful
coppery-orange are borne throughout
summer and autumn. The stems are
rather sparse and need disguising at the
base, but nevertheless this has become a
favourite climber as it is relatively hardy.

Rosa 'Sea Foam'
Modern shrub/weeping
standard/climber
↕ 1m (3ft) ↔ 2m (6½ft)
Hardiness zone: 5
This Australian-bred rose is compact
with old-fashioned shaped, white pearly
flowers. It is frequently grown as ground
cover and sometimes as a small climber.
It repeats well and is best in hot, dry
climates as it does not enjoy rain.

Rosa sericea 'Pteracantha'
Species
↕ 3m (10ft) ↔ 2.5m (8ft)
Hardiness zone: 6
Although this wild rose bears cream
coloured flowers and pretty ferny
foliage, it is grown principally for its
extraordinary, large, flat, blood-red
translucent thorns. With the sun
backlighting the thorns, it makes a
stunning addition to the natural garden.

Rosa 'Sombreuil'
Climbing tea rose
↕ 4m (13ft) ↔ 2m (6½ft)
Hardiness zone: 6
Flesh-pink tinted creamy-white, rosette-
shaped blooms with a strong tea rose
scent, which repeat well throughout
the season. A very hardy old rose.

Rosa 'Veilchenblau'
Multiflora rambler
↕ 3m (10ft) ↔ 2m (6½ft)
Hardiness zone: 5
This thornless rambler is the best known
of the purples; its small, richly orange,
scented flowers are held in bunches,
and can appear blue in certain lights.
It flowers only once early in the season
and is widely grown.

Rosa xanthina 'Canary Bird'
Species
↕ 2.5m (8ft) ↔ 4m (13ft)
Hardiness zone: 5
Bright yellow, single flowers with a light
fruity scent cover this arching shrub.
Delightful ferny leaves borne in tufts
support individual flowers. It makes
an attractive specimen shrub.

Rosa 'Zepherine Drouhin'
Bourbon climber
↕ 3m (10ft) ↔ 2m (6½ft)
Hardiness zone: 5
A reliable hardy climber, which is
thornless with a continuous flower
presence. The fragrant, deep rose-pink
blooms are not particularly special
individually, but are delightful when
seen en masse. It is happy grown on
a cold, shady wall or as a hedge.

Rosa 'Sally Holmes'

Rosa 'Veilchenblau'

Rosa xanthina 'Canary Bird'

Rose Growers and Suppliers

David Austin Roses Ltd
Bowling Green Lane,
Albrighton, Wolverhampton,
England WV7 3HB
01902 376376 tel
01902 375177 fax
&
15059 Highway 64 West
Tyler TX 75704
USA
800 328 8893 toll free tel
903 526 1900 fax
retail@davidaustinroses.com
www.davidaustinroses.com
Breeder of the justly loved 'New
English Roses', with a comprehensive
rose nursery and international mail
order business. Some 700 varieties
of roses planted in their breath-taking
2-acre rose garden.

Peter Beales Roses
London Road, Attleborough
Norfolk, England NR17 1AY
01953 454707
01953 456845
sales@classicroses.co.uk
www.classicroses.co.uk
One of the largest commercially
available collections in the world,
featuring over 1300 varieties of Classic
Roses with over 250 unique to Peter
Beales. The 2.5 acres gardens feature a
magnificent collection of roses.

The City of Blois
Hôtel de Ville
41012 Blois Cedex, France
(33) 02 54 44 50 84
www.ville-blois.fr
Innovative public gardens that include
the Royal Gardens opposite the château,
and the rose terrace at the Bishop's
Palace. Proves the value of forward
thinking local government planning.

The Cranford Rose Garden
Brooklyn Botanic Garden
1000 Washington Avenue
Brooklyn NY 11225, USA
718 623 7200
www.bbg.org
A testament to hard work and the love
of the rose in all its glory, which is also
an educational experience.

Cellars Hohenort Hotel
PO Box 270,
Constantia 7848
Cape Town, South Africa
021 794 2137 tel
021 794 2149 fax
cellars@relaischateaux.com
www.cellars-hohenort.com
Voted one of the top 30 hotel gardens
in the world, these gardens, sitting
adjacent to the Kirstenbosch Botanical
Gardens, are well worth taking time out
to visit when following the wine trail.

**Gardens of the American
Rose Society**
8877 Jefferson Paige Road
Shreveport 71119-8811,
USA
318 938 5402 ext 3011
www.ars.org
The largest park in the US devoted to
America's national flower. Gardens
meander round winding paths, past
fountains, and formal beds.

Hadspen Garden and Nursery
Castle Cary, Somerset,
England BA7 7NG
01749 813707 tel/fax
www.hadspengarden.freeserve.co.uk
Stunning colour in the borders throughout the year with the opportunity to
purchase some very special plants bred
at Hadspen in their nursery.

Il Giardino di Ninfa
04010 località Doganella
Cisterna di Latina,
Italy
0773 632231 tel/fax
Rose covered ruins, and rushing
sparkling waters make this a truly
romantic Italian garden that has inspired
many designers and garden owners.

**Inez Parker Memorial
Rose
Garden**
Park Boulevard at Plaza
de Balboa
San Diego 92101
USA
www.Sandiego.gov/park-and-
recreation
A municpal park designed to be a
model rose garden that would test
the rigours of a public garden open
365 days a year.

La Giardini della Landriana
Via Campo di Carne 51
00040 Tor San Lorenzo,
Ardea,
Italy
06910 14140 tel
06687 2839 fax
Romantic coastal gardens 40k south
of Rome cover 10 hectares divided
into 30 "rooms" many of which feature
old roses.

Les Jardins de l'Alchimiste
Mas de la Brune
13810 Eygalières,
France
(33) 04 90 95 90 77 tel
(33) 04 90 95 99 21 fax
Symbolisim and abstraction in a
contemporary formal setting in
Provence.

Les Jardins de l'Imaginaire

24120 Terrasson, France
05 53 50 30 66 tel
05 53 50 46 76 fax
www.ait-perigord-adapt.com
/terrasson/jardin
A contemporary garden designed as
series of gardens symbolizing man's
links with nature, agriculture, the
garden, and the town.

Les Jardins de Valloires

80120 Argoules, France
02 22 23 53 55 tel
Modern interpretation for the
restoration of the gardens once tended
by Cistercian Monks. Gardens include a
formal rose garden, underplanted with
decorative vegetables.

The Rose Garden

Montreal Botanical Garden
4101 rue Sherbrooke Est
Montreal H1X 2B2, Canada
514 872 1400
Jardin_botanique@ville.
montreal.qc.ca
Designed in 1976, a very modern
design for a rose garden, housing
10,000 roses in its collection, massed
in winding beds in a natural setting
of trees and shrubs.

Nancy Steen Rose Garden

Gladstone Road,
Parnell, Auckland,
New Zealand
09302 1252 tel
09525 5308 fax
Adjacent to the Parnell Rose
Garden, the Nancy Steen Garden
holds a collection of heritage roses in
memory of the gardener who did most
to encourage their preservation and
cultivation in New Zealand.

Ohinetahi

Teddington Road, Governors Bay,
Canterbury, New Zealand
03329 9852 tel/fax
Home of Sir Miles Warren, one of
New Zealand's most significant
private formal gardens, they surround
the historic stone house, They include
a stunning formal rose garden, and
a woodland gully planted with
native plant species.

Roseraie de Berty

07110 Largentière,
France
(33) 04 75 88 30 56 tel
(33) 04 75 88 36 93 fax
Captivating organic gardens
and nursery that specializes in
old roses.

Roseraie de l'Haÿ du Val de Marne

8 rue Albert Watel
94240 l'Haÿ-les-Roses,
France
04 43 99 82 80 tel
04 47 40 04 04 fax
An exceptional formal rose garden –
the world's oldest garden devoted
exclusively to roses.

RHS Garden Hyde Hall

Buckhatch Lane,
Rettendon
Chelmsford, Essex,
England CM3 8ET
01245 400256
www.rhs.org.uk
The latest to be added to the Royal
Horticultural Society's gardens that
numbers two new rose gardens within
its grounds. Becoming renowned for
its rose pruning and training
techniques, demonstrated throughout
the gardens.

Sissinghurst Castle Garden

Sissinghurst, Nr Cranbrook
Kent, England TN17 2AB
01580 710700 tel
01580 710702 fax
Sissinghurst@nationaltrust.org.uk
A 6-acre garden of "outdoor rooms",
created in the 1930 by Vita Sackville-
West, and still considered one of the
most outstanding gardens in England.
Well worth visiting even when crowded.

Tresco Abbey Gardens

Isle of Scilly, Cornwall
England, TR24 0QQ
(44) 01720 424 105
www.tresco.co.uk
The amazing story of how one family
over several generations has created
one of the most incredible "tropical"
gardens where the original concept is
preserved while new ideas are
constantly being introduced.

Wave Hill

675 West 252nd Street, Bronx
New York 10471, USA
www.wavehill.org
28 acres of restored landscaped
gardens looking over the Hudson River
towards the Pallisades. Ongoing
restoration and modernization of the
gardens is continuous, and the results
are awe-inspiring.

Index

Author's acknowledgments

When I was approached to write this book I was considerably surprised by the subject and the title, my first reaction was "we don't use roses in contemporary designs, they've fallen out of fashion in favour of new perennial planting", but I would like to thank Mitchell Beazley in proving my first thoughts incorrect, rekindling my interest in this versatile plant, and being able to explore the work of so many talented designers and diverse gardens. The team at Mitchell Beazley have been patient, helpful, and generous with their time and advice, so my thanks especially to Michèle Byam, Sarah Rock, Helen Taylor, Selina Mumford, Claire Gouldstone, and Giulia Hetherington and all those unseen people in Production in your faith that I could deliver the words. Also to all those designers, photographers, writers and garden owners who have allowed me to feature their unique gardens. And to my clients and contractors who have seen rather too little of me during the creation of this book and last, but not least to my family and friends, who have given me their loving support.

Acknowledgments/Picture Credits

Mitchell Beazley would like to acknowledge and thank the following for kindly supplying images for publication in this book.
Front cover: Garden Exposures Photo Library/Andrea Jones, design: Judith Wise & Juliet McKelvey; **back cover:** Garden Picture Library/Gary Rogers, design: Alison Armour-Wilson; **back flap:** Nicola Stocken Tomkins

1 Le Scanff-Mayer; 2-3 Clive Nichols Garden Pictures/Clive Nichols, design: Alison Armour-Wilson, with David Austin roses, Chelsea 2001; 5 Garden Picture Library/Ron Sutherland; 6 Le Scanff-Mayer; 8 National Trust Photographic Library/Andrew Lawson; 9 Garden Picture Library/Ron Evans; 10 Kate Gadsby; 11 Steven Wooster; 12 Dan Kiley; 13 top Mise au Point/Arnaud Descat; 13 bottom Harpur Garden Library/Jerry Harpur; 14 Buro Kloeg Gardenphotos/Gert Tabak; 15 Buro Kloeg Gardenphotos/D Kloeg; 16, 17, 18-19 Buro Kloeg Gardenphotos/Gert Tabak; 20 Andrew Lawson; 22 Harpur Garden Library/Jerry Harpur, design: Tom Stuart-Smith; 23 Marianne Majerus, design: Tom Stuart-Smith; 24 Harpur Garden Library/Jerry Harpur; 24-25 Andrew Lawson; 26-27 Steven Wooster; 27 Marijke Heuff; 28-29 Harpur Garden Library/Jerry Harpur, design: Annie Fisher; 29 Nicola Browne, design: Dan Pearson; 30-31 Harpur Garden Library/Jerry Harpur; 32-33, 33 Mise au Point/Frederic Didillon; 34, 34-5 Sofia Brignone; 36 top Garden Picture Library/Howard Rice; 36 bottom, 37 Andrew Lawson; 38, 38-39 Sofia Brignone; 40 John Glover; 42 Marianne Majerus; 42-43 Steven Wooster, Stowe, Christchurch, NZ; 44 Mise au Point/Noun; 45 Steven Wooster/Peter Beale Roses; 46 top Garden Picture Library/John Glover; 46 bottom Harpur Garden Library/Marcus Harpur; 47 Andrew Lawson; 48-49 Harpur Garden Library/Jerry Harpur; 50 John Glover; 51 top Garden Picture Library/Neil Holmes; 51 bottom John Glover; 52-53 Marianne Majerus; 53 Dency Kane; 54 John Glover; 55 Andrew Lawson; 56 Le Scanff-Mayer; 58, 59 Marianne Majerus; 60 Andrew Lawson, design: Dan Pearson; 60-61 Marianne Majerus; 62-63 Alex Ramsay; 64-65 Andrew Lawson; 66 Nicola Browne; 67 Garden Picture Library/Howard Rice; 68 Mise au Point/Frederic Didillon; 69, 70-71 Le Scanff-Mayer; 72, 73 Marianne Majerus; 74 top Garden Picture Library/Densey Clyne; 74 bottom, 75 Alex Ramsay; 76, 76-77 Nicola Browne; 78 Alex Ramsay; 80 Steven Wooster; 81 Harpur Garden Library/Jerry Harpur; 82-83, 84 top Harpur Garden Library/Jerry Harpur; 84 bottom Andrew Lawson; 85 Harpur Garden Library/Jerry Harpur; 86 top Garden Picture Library/John Glover; 87 Harpur Garden Library/Jerry Harpur; 88 Octopus Publishing Group Ltd; 89 Vivian Russell; 90-91, 92, 92-3 Alex Ramsay; 94-95, 95, 96, 97 Karen Bussolini; 98 Conde Nast Publications/Keith Scott Morton; 100, 101 Vivian Russell, planting: John Greenlee; 102, 103 Harpur Garden Library/Jerry Harpur; 104 Vivian Russell; 106 left Nicola Stocken Tomkins;106 right Nicola Browne, design: Dan Pearson; 108, 109 Steven Wooster; 110, 111, 112-13 Marianne Majerus; 114, 115 Saxon Holt; 116 Sofia Brignone; 117 Garden Picture Library/Didier Willery; 118 Sofia Brignone; 120, 121 Vincent Motte; 122 Le Scanff-Mayer; 124, 125 Harpur Garden Library/Jerry Harpur; 126 Garden Picture Library/Jerry Pavia; 127 Harpur Garden Library/Jerry Harpur; 128 Nicola Browne; 129 Le Scanff-Mayer; 130 Garden Picture Library/Martine Mouchy; 130-131 Mise au Point/Arnaud Descat; 132, 133 Steven Wooster; 134, 135 Sofia Brignone; 136, 137, 138 Nicola Browne; 140, 141 Greenworld Pictures Inc/Mick Hales; 142, 143 Brooklyn Botanic Garden; 144 Clive Nichols Garden Pictures/Clive Nichols, Chelsea 1998, design: Sarah Raven ; 146 left Octopus Publishing Group/Stephen Wooster; 146 right Octopus Publishing Group; 146 centre Andrew Lawson; 147 left and right Garden Picture Library/John Glover; 148 left Andrew Lawson; 148 right Garden Picture Library/Lamontagne; 149 left Andrew Lawson; 149 right Garden Picture Library/John Glover; 149 centre Octopus Publishing Group; 150 left Andrew Lawson; 150 right Garden Picture Library/Lamontagne; 150 centre Garden Picture Library/Kit Young; 151 left Octopus Publishing Group; 151 right, 152 left and right Andrew Lawson; 152 centre Garden Picture Library/Howard Rice; 153 left Garden Picture Library/Mayer/Le Scanff; 153 right Andrew Lawson; 154 left Octopus Publishing Group; 154 right Garden Picture Library/Densey Clyne; 154 centre Garden Picture Library/Clive Nichols; 155 left and right Andrew Lawson; 155 centre Octopus Publishing Group.